Here is a little book
The Gospel of the K...
shatter paradigms. \
the Kingdom, so the world can see more of the Kingdom of
God in our lives.

Darrow Miller
Co-Founder, Disciple Nations Alliance

Eng Hoe is a talented trainer and community development
practitioner who has a real gift for synthesizing, simplifying
and making practical important ideas. He has done us all a
great service by masterfully weaving together the key
biblical concepts for transformational ministry that have
shaped his own life. This is a highly readable and powerful
book. I heartily recommend it!

Scott Allen
President, International Secretariat,
Disciple Nations Alliance

The Gospel of the Kingdom by Eng Hoe is one of the best
books I've read in recent times. I deeply appreciate the
fearlessness and the forthrightness with which the author
deals with the much neglected subject of love for the poor
and needy. I guarantee that every reader will get a fresh
glimpse into the heart of God.

R. Stanley
A Building Engineer turned Bible Teacher
Founder, Blessing Youth Mission, India

Jesus said, "Any of you who does not give up everything he has cannot be my disciple." The only way any one of us can do this is when we are crazily and hopelessly in love with Jesus. This isn't just another book about poverty or transformation. At its very heart, it is about our romance with the Divine Romancer. Rare. Insightful. Challenging. All Christians should read this book and allow His love to flood us afresh. Only then can we live out the greatest commandment of loving God and our neighbor.

Roxanne Tan
Starfish International Partnerships Coordinator, Singapore.

This is one of those books that I would categorize as a "must read". Having interacted closely with Eng Hoe over the last two years, I have been infected by his passion and I know many others have been too! The time has come for serious Christians to shed their inhibitions and say: "Here I am Lord. I want to be counted among those who love you passionately and love the people you have placed around me – the poor, the marginalized, the sick and the victims of injustice. I want to be the 'good news' to those who crave to see Jesus through the lives of His disciples"

Paul Balasundaram
Former Executive Director, Haggai Institute, India and Starfish Coordinator for India

---

Stalin once said, "The death of one man is a tragedy. The death of millions is a statistic." In his book Eng Hoe manages to turn statistics into tragedies via his personal experiences and his down to earth powerful narrative. Crafted after many years of wide travels, observations, and honest reflections, the author incisively illustrates out of his own experiences primarily in Asia, spiced also by visits to Africa. I would easily add Latin America. But it is not the author's personal experiences that makes the book so powerful, but his solid use of Biblical principles and the abundance of Scripture quoted and overall biblical perspective, amply illustrated.

Eng Hoe basically highlights that the Gospel has eternal but also ongoing – here and now – obligations and dimensions, particularly dealing with our practical actions towards the poor. Say good bye to Plato's dualism and welcome a solid Biblical argument for the recovery of so oft forgotten dimensions of the Gospel and the true nature of the church. We think we might be saved and be on our way to heaven, but we had better not be so sure. The church has a lot of work and deep responsibilities to fulfill en route, and those obligations have to do with the physical and not just the spiritual needs of others. Not doing so would mean we never really had God's love in us and it would be presumptuous to think that we were really advancing to heaven or even advancing at all.

Carlos Calderon
International Director, Partners International

To be concerned about the poor is an important theme of the Bible. In fact some would argue that our concern for the poor is a reflection of our love for God, described in Scripture as 'father of the fatherless and protector of widows.' (Psalm 68:5) Our concern for the poor is a most accurate measure of our spirituality.

Eng Hoe has written a book that will challenge us to re-examine our walk with God. If we really love God, we will love our neighbours, especially those who are in need. He made the thought-provoking point *'that the question of eternal life or salvation is related to loving my neighbor.'* This book does not allow us to hold a 'neutral' position. It forces us to take sides. I believe the question he is asking is, "Are you on the same side as God who is calling His Church to love the poor, a vital expression of the Gospel of the Kingdom?"

The Very Revd Kuan Kim Seng,
Dean, St. Andrew's Cathedral
(Anglican) Diocese of Singapore

"Why, exactly, would the world's richest man, a multi-trillion-billionaire, leave his comfortable world and enter the painful, noisy, hopeless and smelly world of the poor?

Simple. Because Jesus was driven by irrational love. Without love like an ocean, our brain simply cannot grasp nor comprehend the obscene and violent poverty around us – and in the disaster-stricken days to come. Many call for a radical engagement with the poor, because it is the right thing to do, because it is theologically correct, because our guilt and shame tells us. The truth is : you can only change what you love. And love fuels us to do something ultimate, something seriously silly. It propels us to nothing less than to enter the world of the ones we love, while it bursts our fuses and makes us act irrational, very un-German – in the name of the God who loved all of us, in spite of the fact that he knew us!

Eng Hoe has done a great job with this book being a Kingdom tour guide into the world of the poor. So buy ten copies, give it to anyone in whom you spot even an ounce of passion, and meet together soon to plan a loving invasion

of Kingdom passion into a pocket of poverty in your area –
or someplace around the world. Jesus has done it before.
Now it's your turn. "

Wolfgang Simson
Author of 'Houses that Change the World' and 'Starfish
Manifesto'

The Gospel of the Kingdom
– Revealing the Heart of God

Cover Design by Christina Tan

Updated 21 July 2015

The
GOSPEL
of the
KINGDOM

REVEALING THE HEART OF GOD

*"Your Kingdom come, Your will be done,
on earth as it is in heaven"*

Contents

If it can be said that there are certain core truths in the Bible, I believe one of them must be that God is love and that we were made to be like Him, meaning we were made to love.

We become most like Him, most alive, and find our greatest joy and fulfilment when we love – when we feel for others, when we give, and when we bring joy to others and serve others. Not when we are immersed in ourselves, and accumulate, and hoard and serve ourselves.

This is a paradox but the more we seek fulfilment for ourselves, the further we will be from finding it, because the further we will be from what we were created to be. But the more we turn our gaze away from ourselves and love and give and serve, the closer we will be to what we were created to be, and the more we will experience fulfilment.

Preface

Several years ago I went through a paradigm shift that changed the direction of my life. It had to do with two things – my understanding of the Gospel and the poor. This is a short narrative of my journey – from understanding the Gospel as the Gospel of salvation, to understanding it as the Gospel of the Kingdom. From that, my whole understanding of church and missions also went through a radical paradigm shift. In fact, an alternative title to this book could be *'The Gospel of the Kingdom – A Paradigm Shift for the Church'.*

Others who went through this same shift have written "heavy" theological books on it. I have however written this book in simple down-to-earth language in the hope that many will find this quite readable. "The Gospel of the Kingdom" is of course a theme too supreme for a little book like this to do justice to it, but my purpose is not to attempt a treatise on the subject. There is a lot more I would like to share about the Kingdom of God, and expand on each point I've made, but I have intentionally kept this book short, addressing only some core aspects that I believe have been missing from "the Gospel" as normally understood by most Christians.

For easy reading, I have deliberately kept the main message concise within each chapter. The Appendices illustrate and clarify some issues from the main message. Please read the Appendices too or you would not get the full message. The questions at the end of each chapter may be used for your cell group discussions each week. I cannot promise to reply all emails, or reply immediately, but if you are a serious seeker, or a fellow sojourner, I would love to hear from you. May the Lord give us "eyes that see and ears that hear" (Deut.29:4, Prov.20:12) and may our hearts be forever ravished by His love.

Eng Hoe
acts1322@gmail.com
https://acts1322issachar.wordpress.com/

Acknowledgements

This book was born out of a journey of many years of twists and turns. I cannot name all the people who have contributed in one way or another to the many times I have been either touched by their love and faithfulness or pushed out of the box to see things in another light. But special mention must be made of some who have been companions with me on this journey or have influenced me in a profound way : my wife Asha and my children Sarah, Samuel and Zoe my closest companions on this journey, Dr Joseph Paul Ozawa who stood by me in the most trying times and whom I regard as my mentor, Dean Kuan Kim Seng and Peter Dias who have been good friends and a greater encouragement to me than they might realize, and Danis my Papuan friend who loves the poor like no other.

Several writers and teachers have also contributed profoundly to my understanding and journey : AW Tozer, Watchmen Nee, EM Bounds, George Verwer, Gene Edwards, Rick Joyner, Darrow Miller, M Scott Peck, John White, Wolfgang Simson, Ben Wong, Bert Farias, Selwyn Hughes, and Stan Rowland amongst many others.

I am grateful to Ruth and Vishal Mangalwadi for allowing me to reproduce chapter 1 of their book 'William Carey and the Regeneration of India' written so excellently, in Appendix 2 in this book. And thank you Darrow, Scott, Carlos, Kim Seng, Wolfgang, Roxanne, Paul, and R Stanley, people I highly esteem, for your endorsements.

My grateful thanks also to Lynda Johnson for her editing and very helpful suggestions how something might be better phrased. Notwithstanding, at certain points I decided to retain the emphasis I wanted to make, so any flaws that you might come across in the text remain mine. Greg Fritz has also been instrumental in acting as a friendly "fish out of the water" in helping me reflect how I am coming across. And thanks Christina for the nice cover design!

Chapter 1

The Gospel and Poverty

Is it any wonder that many will say to Jesus, "When did we see you hungry .. thirsty .. sick.. naked .. homeless .. in prison?"

My Boat was Rocked … Overturned Actually!

I first visited Bangladesh in 1994. That visit radically changed my understanding of the Gospel. Prior to that, though I live in a developing country, I had never seen such terrible poverty, nor was I aware of the immense poverty in other parts of the world. As I researched the subject of poverty, I discovered that *nearly half of the people in the world, live below the World Bank's poverty line*. (See Appendix 1 on Poverty Statistics). Staggering! And very disturbing. But what has poverty to do with the Gospel? How did the problem of poverty overturn my understanding of the Gospel?

Before my visit to Bangladesh, my understanding of the Gospel was a message of salvation in Jesus Christ. People need to be saved or they will go to hell. So our task is to preach the Gospel and get as many people as possible saved. When I saw the immense poverty in Bangladesh, it made me re-read my Bible. It made me ask, *If our focus is only on getting people saved so that they have an assurance of eternal life in heaven, what about their life on earth?* Jesus said He was anointed to preach the Gospel, the good news, to the poor. What did He tell them? How did He treat them? *What would good news be for the poor?* Is the good news we have for them limited to this – that there is a place in heaven waiting for them, and they will one day be free from their poverty when they die, but meanwhile they just have to suffer it out here on earth?

I was very troubled by these questions. Does God not love them and care for their suffering and misery? What I saw broke my heart. I reasoned that surely God loves them infinitely more than I do. I could not imagine that their suffering did not break the heart of God. The very first thing Jesus said when He started His ministry was, *"The Spirit of the Lord is on me, because he has anointed me to proclaim good news to the poor. He has sent me to proclaim freedom for the prisoners and recovery of sight for the blind, to set the oppressed free, to proclaim the year of the Lord's favor."* (Luke 4:18-19). Yet why was it that the church did not seem to have any good news for the poor about their physical suffering? Not only that, why was it that the church hardly showed any concern or even talked about poverty?

How have We Responded to Poverty?

Every day 35,000 children die of hunger-related causes or lack of basic sanitation and clean water. Imagine that – EVERY DAY! Every year more than 1 million children are forced into the sex trade. Isn't that heart breaking? Nearly half the population of the world lives in slums. Have you ever walked through a slum in Mumbai, Manila, Jakarta or Johannesburg? Or through a village on the outskirts of any city in most of Southeast Asia, South Asia and Africa?

Consider also how poverty breeds sickness and disease, bribery and corruption, gambling, prostitution, street gangs, theft, terrorism, drugs, human trafficking, domestic violence, child abuse, alcoholism, etc. and the resulting untold deaths, suffering and misery. If you know people who work among the poor, they will tell you not only of hunger and want, but also of dysfunctional families, chaotic relationships, and unnecessary tragedies like what I heard happened recently in a village in Indonesia. A little girl, only 5 years old, had an eye infection. Her uneducated father, desiring to help his daughter but having no money for a doctor visit, tried to cure the infection by pouring kerosene into her eye. She was blinded for life.

How have we, the church, the people of God, responded to the misery and suffering of the world? The answer and the statistics are even more staggering and shocking than the statistics on poverty. Did you know that 96% of all money given in church remains in the church and less than 1% goes to the poor? And in terms of global Christian income, less than 0.01% or 0.0001 goes to the poor (See Appendix 1). What does this tell us about ourselves and our understanding of the Gospel? Does it not tell us that either we do not care, or that in our understanding, the Gospel has nothing to do with the health and well-being of people?

Why are Poverty and its Related Problems Not Addressed in Church?

I once gave a message about poverty at a national missions conference. At the end of the message, an elderly gentleman asked a question. He said, "I have been an elder of the church for more than 38 years of my life. I have heard thousands of sermons in my lifetime. Yet I have never ever heard the message you just gave, or anything about poverty. Why is that?" He had a very troubled look on his face. In reply I asked him, "Sir, first of all, I need to ask you, is there anything I have said that is not biblical?" He thought about it for a moment and replied, "No, there is nothing you said that is not biblical. In fact everything you said is biblical and so true and so vital, yet it is never preached in church … Why is that?"

He had a good question. Why do we have so little, in fact almost no concern for the poor? Neither are we much concerned for the other poverty-related problems of corruption, child abuse, human trafficking, etc. When was the last time you heard, or have you ever heard, a message on these issues in church? How much, if at all, has the church gotten involved in addressing these issues? We are happily busy with our church programs while all around us the ills and diseases of society are crippling millions and bringing this world to the brink of collapse, but it doesn't seem to concern us. Why is that?

Does our Gospel have no answers for the plight of the poor?

In reply to that question from the church elder, I said, "With all due respect sir, actually the one who should answer this question is you, not me. When you started becoming an elder of the church, I was still a kid running around in shorts." For a moment he was quiet. Then he had another question, "Tell me, have you given this message in other churches and what happened after you spoke?" "Yes," I said, "I have spoken about this in many churches and meetings. What happened each time was what will happen after this meeting. Some of you will come and tell me what a good speaker I am and what a challenging message it was, and you will thank me for the message. Then next week you will look for another good speaker with another good message. That's all. In other words, nothing happened." Silence filled the room. Quickly the chairman of the meeting came forward looking quite embarrassed and promptly ended the meeting. Guess what happened after that? Exactly what I said!

Before I get back to address the question of whether our Gospel has any answers for the plight of the poor, let me digress and talk a little bit about paradigm shifts because what I went through – and what I believe the church needs `to go through – is a paradigm shift in our understanding of the Gospel.

For small group discussion :

1. What are your experiences with the poor?
2. What good news did you have for the poor?
3. Have you ever felt God's heart for the poor, or been disturbed by the poverty (or any of its related issues) in this world?
4. How has your church addressed issues of poverty and the Gospel's relation to poverty?
5. Why do you think nothing happened after the churches heard the message on poverty and God's love for the poor?

Chapter 2

Get Ready to be Rocked .. or Overturned!

What happens when one has striven long and hard to develop a working view of the world, a seemingly useful, workable map, and then is confronted with new information suggesting that that view is wrong and the map needs to be largely redrawn?

⁃ Scott Peck, *The Road Less Traveled*

Paradigm Shifts

Paradigm shifts are not an easy thing to make. Three examples come to mind. When man first discovered that the earth is spherical in shape, not flat, it came as a complete shock to most people. They could not accept it. Their eyes told them otherwise. It took a long time for many people to embrace that. Some refused to accept it no matter what scientific evidence was presented to them. Even today, some people refuse to accept it. Such people formed a society called the "Flat Earth Society" that still existed at the start of the 20th century.

Another example is the story of Galileo's discovery of gravitational force. Imagine if we drop a table, a chair, a piece of chalk, and a book from a 5th storey balcony all at the same time. Which do you think would hit the ground first? This is one of the crazy things we did as students. In his experiment Galileo dropped two objects of different weights from a height and found that they hit the ground at the same time. Legend has it that he demonstrated this at the famous Tower of Pisa in Italy and invited university professors and leaders in the city to witness it. But they refused to even entertain the idea that that could be true and so they refused to go and watch him demonstrate it.

After we learned about Galileo's experiment, a few of us decided to try it for ourselves after school hours, when no teachers were watching! Guess what -- we discovered *for ourselves* that Galileo was right. And we took pride in the fact that we knew it by experience, whereas our Physics teacher knew it only in theory. (Or maybe he had tried it himself when he was a student! ☺)

Another example is how it appears to us that the sun is revolving around the earth, when in fact it is the earth that is rotating on its own axis (which is why we have day and night) and the earth is revolving around the sun.

A clear case of a paradigm shift in the Bible was when Jesus was crucified and resurrected. The disciples' idea of their Messiah was that he would lead them to overcome the Roman Empire and establish his rule on earth. They were totally devastated when Jesus did not defend himself but surrendered and died at the hands of Roman soldiers. That forced a paradigm shift on them. When Jesus came back to life, they went through another paradigm shift about their Messiah and his mission.

Another paradigm shift took place after they experienced Pentecost. They saw themselves with a totally new identity and mission. Later, Peter and the early church went through yet another paradigm shift in their understanding of God's plans – that the good news was not only for the Jews but also for the Gentiles. Even then, they were still stuck in Jerusalem (another Old Testament paradigm) for another 25 years, notwithstanding that Jesus had told them to go to the ends of the earth. Imagine, Paul, who wasn't one of the original 12 who received the command, goes out 3 times spanning possibly more than 15 years and each time he returns, the original 11 are still stuck in Jerusalem! What on earth was going on in the minds of the 11 apostles? Finally, when the Romans ransacked Jerusalem in AD 70, they had yet another paradigm shift forced on them.

God's Purposes Advance through Paradigm Shifts

Paradigm shifts require a death to long held (even sacrosanct) ideas first, before we are ready to embrace new ideas that contradict our old long-held ideas. The Jewish religious leaders in Jesus' days refused to do that. Jesus said new wine cannot be put into old wineskins. You need new wineskins for new wine. It is not easy for people to give up long-held ideas. Jesus also said that those who have drunk the old wine don't want the new. They will say the old is better. Such is our human nature. We are naturally resistant to change. It is therefore not surprising that there are numerous examples of paradigm shifts in the Bible.

Each key person who was instrumental in God's agenda had to go through radical paradigm shifts before God's purposes could advance through him or her: Job, Abraham, Jacob, Joseph, Moses, David, Mary the mother of Jesus, Peter and all the disciples, Paul, etc. It is evident as history unfolded, that for God's purposes to take place, each step, each advance, required a paradigm shift of his people. We may think we have already understood God's ways and his plans and purposes, but guess what – they are always far bigger and greater than our narrow minds can comprehend.

I believe the church badly needs a paradigm shift in its understanding of the Gospel that will lead to a paradigm shift in our understanding of our role, of God's mission for us, in this world. When that happens, it would also lead us to a paradigm shift in our understanding and practice of church – *from church as we know it, to church as God wants it* (a phrase borrowed from Wolfgang Simson, the author of

"Houses that Change the World" and "Starfish Manifesto"). In fact what is needed is an overturning of almost everything that we have come to know as Christianity.

Jesus Came to Turn Everything Upside Down

This world is a runaway world. From the time of Adam and down through history, man has declared his independence from God and set up his own kingdoms in opposition to God's Kingdom (more on this in Chapter 7). Throughout the Bible we see that much of what this world values, God considers rubbish and foolishness. Conversely, much of what is regarded as rubbish and foolishness by this world, God values. One of the key issues is how the world treats the poor. When Jesus came, He turned everything upside down. He denounced the rich and powerful (Lk.6:24-25) and lifted up the poor, the nobodies, and the rejects of society. Look at how He lived with the poor and how He treated them. He identified so much with them that He said whatever we do for them, we have done it for Him (Matt.25:31-46). By His own birth and death, the King of Glory not only identified with the poor, He exemplified this reversal.

At the very start of His mission, Jesus said He was anointed to bring good news to the poor (Lk.4:18). What is the good news? The good news is the Kingdom (Lk.9:2,6). He also said the Kingdom belongs to the poor (Matt.5:3, Lk.6:20) and to those who serve them (Matt.25:34). This surely is good news to the poor. But why does the Kingdom belong to the poor? What about the rich? Basically Jesus told the poor that while the rich and powerful who rule this world may have oppressed and rejected them, while the world has marginalized them and forgotten about them, God is for them (Lk.4:18-19, Matt.5:3-6). One day when Jesus returns, the big shots, the rich, and the powerful will be cast out.

The nobodies and rejects of society will rule with Him (Jas.2:5, Lk.1:52, 1 Sam.2:7-8, Lk.16:19-26).

There is another more fundamental reason why the Kingdom belongs to the poor. Wolfgang Simson has said it so well : for God's Kingdom to come, man's kingdom must go. God's Kingdom can reign only in those who are humble, or who are poor in spirit (who are broken and contrite within : Isa.57:15, Isa.66:1-2). For those who have been rejected by the kingdoms of this world, God's Kingdom is obviously good news. It is however bad news for the rich who are to give up their wealth and share it with the poor (Lk.18:23-25). It can't be very good news either for those who have kingdoms to surrender. Here then is a question that must confront each of us : Do we really want to be part of God's Kingdom? Do read on if you are ready for your boat to be rocked .. or overturned!

For small group discussion :

1. Have you ever experienced a paradigm shift? What was it that caused you to have that shift?
2. Why do you think the apostles remained in Jerusalem for 25 years despite having been commanded by Jesus to be His witnesses in Jerusalem, Judea, Samaria and to the uttermost parts of the earth?
3. What do you think are the old wineskins of the church today?
4. What do you think is the difference between God's Kingdom and the kingdoms of this world?
5. What has the Gospel to do with the issues and problems of life in this world?

Chapter 3

Good News for the Poor

Imagine if you were in misery and someone came and told you he has good news for you. He tells you that if you would become a Christian everything will be good and fine after you die, but he does nothing to help you. How would that be good news to you?

Does Our Gospel have No Answers for the Plight of the Poor?

The common understanding of Christians is that the Gospel is a message of salvation in Jesus that everyone should know. The goal of the church is to try and get as many people as possible into heaven. If indeed that is all there is about the Gospel, then we have no solutions and no answer for the problem of poverty, *or any other problems in this world*. If salvation from this world is all we are concerned with, and we have no concern with what goes on in this world, doesn't that make us irrelevant, powerless and ineffective in this world?

After my time in Bangladesh, as I re-read my Bible, it was like I had just put on a fresh pair of spectacles. I began to see things that have always been there but had somehow missed previously. I realized that I had been seeing and understanding the Gospel from a very limited perspective, to such an extent that I had almost completely misunderstood the Gospel. No doubt salvation is a fundamental part of the Gospel, but I discovered that it is only a part. Not all there is to the Gospel. There is so much more to the Gospel that I had not realized. It was not a deeper theology of salvation that I needed, but rather a larger scope of the Gospel. In fact what I needed was ... yes ... a paradigm shift. I was missing the big picture, or as the English would say, "Missing the wood (forest) for the trees." I had to step back and see the enormity of the forest. When I came to realize the enormity of the Gospel, it radically changed my whole approach to missions and to the poor.

Over the last 20 years my involvement with crisis relief and community development has taught me that the Gospel is not only a message of good news to get us into heaven, but also good news that we can be part of God's Kingdom on earth which involves living whole and fulfilling lives here on earth. God is concerned for the whole person, not just his spirit and soul, not just his eternal salvation but also his whole being here on earth. And God is not only concerned for what is happening on earth in our lives, *He sends us and expects us to be agents of change and transformation in this world*. And we do indeed have good news for the poor. I'll come to that in a moment. But first, let's get to the heart of the matter.

As I travel around the world teaching and training, I keep coming across more and more people who are catching the vision or "drift" of trying to get the church out of its four walls to engage in social concern. That is wonderful. However, I find that much of such efforts are only introducing yet more program and activity into the church to make church more interesting, without getting to the heart of the matter. *Instead, what we need is a radical shift in our understanding of the Gospel and of our identity – of who we, the church, are to be in this world, of who and what God intended us to be in this world*. Unless we do, we will be falling far short of God's Kingdom mandate for us.

What is the Gospel? Let's Hear it from Jesus Himself

Imagine if someone came up to you one day and asked you what he had to do in order to be saved. What would you tell him? You would tell him the Gospel. We may express it in different ways, but basically you would tell him something like this - that he could not justify himself, that he could not work for his salvation, that he could only depend on and trust in Jesus' atoning death to be accepted as righteous before God, that in order to do that he needed to confess his sins and accept Jesus as his Savior and Lord, then his sins would be forgiven and his name would be written in the book of life and he would have eternal life and be assured of a place in heaven when he dies.

My basic understanding of the Gospel was smashed one day by a passage in the Gospels. In Luke 10:25-37, there is a record of a dialogue between an expert in the law and Jesus, that we rarely ever consider in our understanding of what is required for someone to be saved. The expert in the law asked, *"What must I do to inherit eternal life?"* That is no doubt the same as asking what is required for someone to be saved. The answer Jesus acknowledged as correct was not the confession of sins and acceptance of Him as our savior, etc. Rather, it was *to love God with all our heart, soul, mind and strength and to love our neighbor as ourselves*. Yes, this is from the Savior Himself.

The requirement to love God totally, or total surrender to the Lordship of Christ, was not what shook me. I had already known that the word "believe" in John 3:16, in the original Greek, is *"pisteuo"*, and that *"pisteuo"* was not simply a mental assent and acceptance of something to be true, but a total trust and abandonment of oneself upon the object of the belief. The word "faith", in the Greek is *"pistis"*, the noun of *"pisteuo"* and meant the same thing. True faith therefore is a return to what God originally designed for us – a life of total dependence upon God where we are no longer our own god, but we live in total submission to Him as God. Thus a person would not perish but have eternal life only if he believed in Jesus in the sense of surrendering totally to Him. Jesus said that unless a man forsake all he cannot be His disciple (Lk.14:33). (See Appendix 5).

I had already been teaching about total surrender to Jesus. But what shook me was the part about loving my neighbor as myself. I knew that I must love my neighbor, but I had not seen this previously – *that the question of eternal life or salvation is related to loving my neighbor.* What does our salvation have to do with loving our neighbors? Why does our salvation have anything to do with loving our neighbors? Is it not enough just to trust in Jesus for our salvation? Was Jesus making this an additional requirement to what He told Nicodemus in Jn.3:16? How do we reconcile what Jesus said in Lk.10:25-37 with what He said in Jn.3:16?

As I looked more carefully into this, I came to see that there is actually no inconsistency between what Jesus said in Lk.10:25-37 and in Jn.3:16. Neither is loving God and loving our neighbor an additional requirement to Jn.3:16. Allow me to explain. There are two things in Jn.3:16 that are commonly misunderstood : "believe" and "eternal life". "Believe" in Jn.3:16 as I mentioned above, is *pisteuo,* which is actually about total surrender. Not just about trusting in Jesus to save us. I also saw that "eternal life" is about being one with God; not just about living forever in heaven. In Jn.17:3, in His prayer to His Father, Jesus said, *"This is eternal life, that they may know you the only true God and Jesus Christ whom you have sent."* Eternal life was described by Jesus not in terms of length of time, but as "knowing" (Greek : *ginosko*) God. That is the same Greek word used in the Septuagint (the Greek Old Testament) for how Adam knew Eve his wife. In other words, eternal life is being united with God and becoming one with Him (see 1 Cor.6:16-17). So in effect what Jesus said in Jn.3:16 is that whoever would return to God and surrender his life totally to Him, shall not be separated from Him but shall become united (become one) with Him. It begins in this life and carries into the next.

What happens if we are one with God? If we would become one with God, then we would feel what's on His heart and we would love as He loves. So then what Jesus said in Lk.10:25-37 is really no different from what He said in Jn.3:16. Who are those who are truly born again and have eternal life? Those who are united with God. Being united with God, they will love as He loves. Love for others is thus the evidence of a truly born again person (see 1Jn.3:14-19). It is no use for someone to insist he is born again and saved just because he "accepted" Jesus as his savior. The Jews kept claiming they were chosen and saved but Jesus told them that a tree is known by its fruit. Matt.25:31-46 on the sheep and goats confirms to us who are actually born again and who are not. In the end Jesus will divide between those who were truly His sheep (who knew His heart and loved as He loved) and those who were the goats (those who did not). See further discussion in Appendix 5.

It must be understood that Jesus did not come just to save us from hell, nor just so that we will go to church every Sunday. There has to be a reversal or an undoing of what happened in the Garden of Eden (see Appendix 5). He came to save us from living a self-centered life to living a Christ-centered life. In fact it is because we are living a self-centered life that we are separated from God and we are going to hell. This self-centeredness comes from the sin nature that we inherited from Adam and Eve. What is a Christ-centered life? If Christ is the center of our lives then His love in us will compel us to lay down our lives for others just as He did (1Jn.3:16).

The mistake most Christians make about the gospel and about salvation is well illustrated in Lk.10:25-37. It is one of those fundamental paradigm shifts we need to make – to see things from God's perspective and not from our perspective. The expert in the law wanted to be sure about his salvation. He wanted to make sure he fulfilled whatever duty or obligation was required of him to be saved. If he had to love his neighbor as himself, he wanted to be clear about that. So like a typical lawyer (I was one for 10 years!) who needs a precise definition for everything, he asked Jesus, "Who is my neighbor?" In response, Jesus told him the parable of the Good Samaritan, and asked him in return, *"Who do you think was a neighbor to the man in need?"* Instead of defining his legal obligations and his religious duties, Jesus put the man in need in the center and focused on the man in need – *who was a neighbor to him*?

Stop and reflect on this for a moment. What is the difference between the lawyer's question and Jesus' question? It reveals two paradigms of spirituality – the false is contrasted with the true. This rough sketch might perhaps help us see it more clearly :

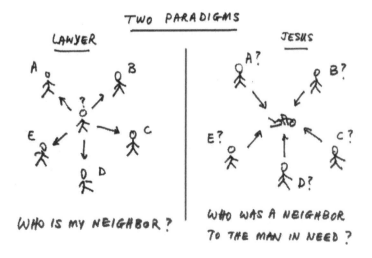

Why did the lawyer ask the question, "Who is my neighbor?" Was the lawyer concerned about others around him? No he was not. He was focused on his own salvation. If he had to love his neighbor, it was in order that he might be saved. It was about gaining merits for his own salvation. It was not about the welfare of his neighbor. But Jesus approached the question of salvation from another paradigm – from the point of view of the man in need. Who was a neighbor to him? Jesus was not concerned about legalistic definitions, boundaries, obligations and religious duties which reveal a wrong understanding of spirituality. Jesus was addressing issues of the heart. What does our life show? How have we been towards people in need? Do we even have eyes to see?

Obviously Jesus told the parable to expose this wrong understanding that the lawyer had, and indeed most Christians have, of salvation and of spirituality. Why didn't the priest and levite stop to help? The man who was robbed was going from Jerusalem to Jericho. The priest and levite passed by on the other side, meaning they were going in the opposite direction. Where were they going? They were probably on their way to worship in Jerusalem and did not want to be late for their worship. Obviously they considered that to be more important than stopping to help the man in need.

Like the expert in the law, and the priest and levite, we too can have a false understanding of spirituality. To most Christians spirituality is an inner focus on oneself. So we focus on building ourselves up spiritually with prayer, worship, Bible study, attending church meetings, etc. Through the parable, however, Jesus tells us that true spirituality is exemplified in the love showed by the non-religious Samaritan. True spirituality is not a focus on oneself, but a focus and concern for others. True spirituality is love. And it is those who love who have eternal life.

Here's something else to think about. Doesn't the question "Who is my neighbor?" sound very much like the question that many ask of God, "What do you want me to do?" or "What is your will for my life?" Instead of asking this question within the 4 walls of our church buildings or within the confines of our comfortable homes, why not get out there to see the needs around us? And ask God to give us eyes to see. And then ask ourselves, "Am I being a neighbor to those in need?"

Part of the reason why I had misunderstood, and I believe that many Christians still misunderstand the gospel is because we are locked in to this idea of "personal salvation", and so we see salvation as a very personal thing that does not involve others. But the gospel is not just good news that I can be saved. Jesus called it the good news of the Kingdom. The good news of the Kingdom is that we can be reconciled to God and we can enter into and become a part of God's Kingdom. What does it mean to be in God's Kingdom? It is to die to self, to be born again, to become one with God, to have His Spirit and His love in us, and to love as He loves. In our own kingdom, it is "I", "Me" and "Myself". But in God's Kingdom, we are no longer focused on ourselves. We are no longer self-centered. We become "other-centered".

When I came to see this, it at the same time answered my question how the gospel would be good news for the poor. If in God's Kingdom we love our neighbors as we love ourselves, then that must be good news for the poor. My eyes were opened to see that God's love for the poor and His answer for their suffering has always been in His Word – we are to be His channel of love and blessing to them! *This is the good news we would have for them, that God does indeed love them and care for them – not only their spiritual but also their physical condition, and He has sent us to love them! And therefore we would love them like we love ourselves, and we would take them into our hearts and share what we have with them like they are our own family!*

But is that the good news we have been giving them? Why are we not part of the good news that we preach? Could it be because we have been brought up in western secular education where truth is understood to be objective, and does not involve us personally? *Could it also be that we have not understood that the gospel has to do with being part of God's Kingdom of love, and not just about being saved from hell?*

For small group discussion :

1. What is your understanding of the Gospel?
2. The author said that Jesus came to save us from living a self-centered life to living a Christ-centered life. What is a Christ-centered life? Consider Gal.2:20 and 1 Jn.3:16
3. Why do you think Jesus addressed the need to believe in Him and be born again with Nicodemus but not with others?
4. Why did Jesus shift the focus of the expert in the law from himself (who is my neighbor?) to others in need (who was neighbor to the one in need?) ?
5. How might these passages be related to each other :
   a) "a tree is known by its fruit" (Matt.7:19-23)
   b) "whoever does not love does not know God" (1 Jn.4:8)
   c) eternal life is knowing God and Jesus Christ (Jn.17:3)
   d) loving God and loving neighbor (Lk.10:25-37)
   e) the parable of the sheep and goats (Matt.25:31-46)
   f) "if any man remain in me and I in him he will bear much fruit" (Jn.15:5)

Chapter 4

Have We Divorced Ourselves from Life Itself?

Why did God create us? Why did He put us on this planet? Did God put us on this planet to save us from this planet?

Spirituality – Individual and Private?

I was a typical evangelical. I was also a typical charismatic, which in some ways made me have an even more lop-sided view of spirituality. Reflecting on my own theology, I have come to realize that spirituality among evangelicals and especially among charismatics is rarely understood or expressed to include love and concern for others. Spirituality is understood only on the individual and personal level/context. Spirituality is individualistic – private daily devotions, understanding of spiritual things, praying in tongues, etc. Spirituality is hardly ever understood in the context of the needs of others in the world. Yet I did not reflect on this until much later (after Bangladesh), that the greatest commandment includes both loving God and loving our neighbors (Matt.22:36-40). The greatest commandment must surely have something to say about what true spirituality is, if not being the yardstick or measure of spirituality?

Spiritual v. Non-Spiritual?

As Bryant Myers and others have pointed out, I think as evangelicals we commonly view the spiritual world as an interior private place and the spiritual realm as confined to the inner invisible life. Somehow we focus only on this spiritual world, while we leave the state and other human institutions to assume responsibility for what happens in everyday life. Our understanding of the Gospel has its focus on eternity and has little to do with politics, economics and social issues of the world around us. From this viewpoint it does not appear to provide answers for the present. What are the consequences of that? Well, it is no wonder that the world thinks we are inadequate and irrelevant. I think we have failed to be salt and light in our communities largely because of our lop-sided theology differentiating between what is "spiritual" and what is "non-spiritual" and focusing only on what we consider as "spiritual".

As I re-read the Bible with a new perspective, I saw that the Bible did not have this differentiation. I reflected on how Jesus was concerned for people, not only for their spiritual condition but also their physical, mental, emotional and social needs. I also reflected on what love is – love is to have someone's welfare in priority to my own. And God showed how He loves us when He sacrificed Himself for us (Jn.15:12-13, 1 Jn.3:16. 1 Jn.4:10).

Then I reflected on how we love our children. We never differentiate between the spiritual and the non-spiritual in our love for our children. It never occurs to us that food, clothing, education, etc. for our children are not so important; but Sunday school and going to church are more important, right? Whatever it may be, we want the best for our children – be it food, clothing, education, friends, etc. How does God love us? Doesn't He want the best for us? So what makes us think that God would regard the spiritual as more important and the physical, mental, emotional and social as less important?

Whose idea was it – was it the devil or was it God who created us with a body? Are our body, mind and emotions inherently sinful or is it the sinful nature that we inherited from Adam that is sinful? I believe the apostle Paul made that sufficiently clear in Romans 6, 7 and 8. There is nothing inherently sinful in our body, mind or emotions. We can choose whether to give in to the desires of our Adamic/sinful nature or to submit to God and keep dedicating ourselves (spirit, body, mind, emotions) to Him and follow His desires.

Does God Not Care for Our Physical Needs?

Didn't Jesus say that we should not worry about what we would eat and what we would wear? Oh yes He did. But on re-reading the whole passage in Matthew and Luke which culminates in, *"But seek first His kingdom and His righteousness, and all these things will be given to you as well."* (Matt.6:33), I came to realize that it is easy to read that out of context and misunderstand what Jesus was talking about.

Jesus was not saying that all these things are not important, or of little importance, or that the spiritual should take priority over the physical, but that we should not let these things distract us from giving ourselves totally to seeking and pursuing His Kingdom. There is nothing inherently evil or bad in the physical or material. The problem is not in the physical or material things themselves. Materialism is in the heart and mind of a person. The problem is the fear (of not having enough) and greed (for more) in us that makes us so focused on material things. But if we know God as our Father and trust Him, we need not be like the pagans who do not know God but have to strive on their own and chase after these things (Matt.6:32). If we would focus on God's Kingdom and give ourselves to being agents of His Kingdom advance, then we need not worry ourselves about these things because He would take care of all these things so that we can get on with our task. It is something like a "You take care of my business and I will take care of yours" kind of deal. Jesus said if God takes care of the sparrows and the flowers, how much more us, since we are so much more precious to Him. That clearly means that God considers our physical needs as important. *And He certainly wasn't telling us that we should not be concerned about whether <u>others</u> had enough to eat or wear.*

What about the verse, *"Do not love the world or anything in the world. If anyone loves the world, love for the Father is not in them. For everything in the world—the lust of the flesh, the lust of the eyes, and the pride of life—comes not from the Father but from the world. The world and its desires pass away, but whoever does the will of God lives forever"* (1 Jn.2:15-17)?

Was John telling us that God is not concerned about our physical needs or that it is sinful to be concerned about physical needs? Certainly not. John was warning us against worldliness, which is an obsession and pursuit of things to satisfy our human lusts and ego; not that there is anything intrinsically evil in material things. We are not to get caught up in the spirit or current of this world; but it does not mean that God is not concerned for the basic needs of people. God Himself loves the world, not worldliness. Meaning, the people of this world. That's why He sent His Son. And when Jesus came, he said the thief comes to steal, kill and destroy, but He had come that we can have abundant life (Jn.10:10). *And John was certainly not telling us that we should not be concerned for the physical needs of others.* In fact, in his epistle we all know that he considered those who said they loved God but did not love the person in need standing in front of them, as fakes.

What is Abundant Life?

I often ask this question in the training I give on Community Development/Transformation for the poor. Jesus came that we might have abundant life. But what is "abundant life?" In one of the trainings in India, someone answered, "Air-conditioning!" and everyone laughed. In quick response, someone else among the participants immediately said, "Hey that's materialism, not abundant life. When Jesus was talking about abundant life, he was talking about our spiritual life." To my surprise, many participants nodded in agreement. So I said, "You mean it is materialism for them but not materialism for us? Meaning, it is not ok for the poor to have air-conditioning, but it is ok for us?" Why is it that many people who are well off seem to have this idea that they are entitled to be well off but somehow there are others who are not equally entitled, or who are meant to be poor?

Let's take the argument further. If air-conditioning is materialistic, what about fans? What determines that air-conditioning is materialistic but fans are not? Have you ever been in a village where a fan would be considered a luxury that only the rich could own? Did you know there are hundreds of thousands, possibly millions of such villages in the world that not only have no fans, but no electricity? If the majority in the world do not even have fans, and we who have fans are the rich (and materialistic?) minority, should we stop using our air-conditioners and fans as well?

Few of us living in cities in more developed nations are aware that possibly more than half the world's population live in places where the temperature in summer can average more than 42⬚ C / 107.6⬚ F, and it is like you are living in an oven, and a fan will only circulate hot air. How should we regard air-conditioning in these places? Still a luxury and materialistic? Where do you draw the line? At what temperature would air-conditioning and fans not be regarded as a luxury and materialistic? And what about heating for winter?

What about education and good roads and good public transport? Have they nothing to do with abundant life? What about uninterrupted water and electricity supply? What about sanitation and garbage disposal? What about access to information and good clean government and ethical business practices? What about work and income to feed our children? What about schools and universities, and banks that you can trust? What about planes that don't drop from the sky and air traffic control that is efficient and reliable? I have a story to tell you about this one!

Planes that Don't Drop from the Sky

I was once in a meeting in the US where a professor of theology had just returned from a trip around India and he gave a talk on what the Gospel is. It was obvious he was very disappointed with what he saw in India. In summary, he said many ministries in India had deviated from the pure message of the Gospel into social concern and they should get back to preaching salvation. I understood where he was coming from, but he was overemphasizing his case to the extent that he said all these social concern activities are not part of the Gospel. In response I wanted to ask him a few questions after he finished but I never got the chance to. I would have asked him, "How did you get to India – did you swim there or take a plane? And when you were about to land, did you have to worry if there was any air traffic control or if they knew what they were doing? Did you even wonder if there was an adequate runway? Weren't you glad that it was because the early missionaries understood the Gospel to include education that they started schools (amongst many other things), and that was how development took place in India, and that ensured you of a safe landing at the airport?" (See Appendix 2)

If the abundant life that Jesus was talking about does not include education and literacy and computers, would I even be able to communicate with you and would you even be able to read this? If abundant life does not have to do with any of these things, why are we enjoying these things then? Do we have a scriptural basis for all these things? If not, why not take our children out of school and pack up and we all go and live in the wilderness?

Or let me put the question across in a different way. There are many nations in the world where their governments are not only totally corrupt but totally inept and incompetent and almost everything in the nation is mismanaged and in chaos – where garbage is strewn all over the place, and people have to live, not only without regular electricity and water supply and proper educational and health facilities, and many people have no work and income to feed their families, but they also live in fear of street crimes and gang violence all the time. Imagine living there. Would living in such environment be considered "abundant life"?

Please understand that I am talking about abundant life on earth so that we understand that it is not confined to the "spiritual". And I am talking about abundant life for the poor. I am not talking about abundant life in terms of what has become known as the "prosperity gospel" – of becoming materially rich and getting more "blessings" for ourselves – a distorted teaching which has infected so many so-called "charismatic" churches today and that is being craftily employed by an increasing number of "pastors" in Asia and Africa to enrich themselves.

For small group discussion :

1. How does the "private" concept of spirituality and the spiritual/non-spiritual dichotomy make us irrelevant to this world?
2. Read the Poverty Statistics in Appendix 1. How can Matt.6:33 be reconciled with Jn.10:10 and the immense poverty and social needs of the world?
3. Did Jesus tell us not to be concerned with whether others have enough to eat and wear? Why is spirituality and "love not the world" usually understood to mean that we should not to have anything to do with the affairs of this world or have any role in changing the world?
4. What would abundant life be for the poor and needy?
5. Read Appendix 2. What do you think was William Carey's understanding of the Gospel?

Chapter 5

Love is About Others

"Of all the earthly music, that which reaches farthest into heaven is the beating of a truly loving heart."

⯃ *Henry Ward Beecher*

What About … Others?

If you have been a Christian for some time and you have been reading your Bible, you would no doubt know that Jesus came not only to save us, but He also came to set us free from legalism. And you would also know that materialism is not in the things we possess but in our hearts. Some people would say we need to distinguish between needs and wants. Yes, that might be helpful, but I think even that is not the real issue. I believe, after we read Jesus', Paul's and John's teaching, we will understand it is not a question of measuring ourselves in relation to certain criteria. The real issue and the real test of spirituality is not how much we fast and pray, or how much Scripture we know, or how much evangelism we do, but how we are in our hearts *towards God and towards others*. In other words, do we love people, especially those in need? If we do, how should we live our lives in relation to them? Like, do we love God? If we do, how should we live our lives in relation to Him?

We know what we have been saved from, but what have we been saved to? Why is it that most Christians are focused only on being *saved from* .. and no one is asking what they are *saved to?* So we keep telling unbelievers that they must accept Christ to be saved from hell. And Christians are very happy that they have been saved from hell. But what are we saved to? By the way, is it conceptually possible that one can be saved from something but not saved to something?

As I pointed out in chapter 3, the other half of the truth that seems to have escaped most Christians is that Jesus did not come to just save us from hell, but to save us from a self-centered life. In fact it is because we are living a self-centered life that we are separated from God and we are going to hell. So what then are we saved to? We are saved to enter into His Kingdom. What does it mean to be in God's Kingdom? It is back to the parable of the Good Samaritan (Lk.10:25-37). And the parable of the sheep and goats (Matt.25:31-46). How are we loving others, especially the poor and needy?

Imagine if Jesus were to show up at your Sunday service and start dividing the sheep and the goats. How many of us would be found to be sheep? When was the last time we showed love to a hungry, thirsty, homeless, sick, naked, or lonely person? The average Christian is so far from having anything to do with the poor that in all likelihood hardly one person in a congregation would be able to recall a time in which he did. Jesus made it clear that to the "goats" the King will say, *"Depart from me, you who are cursed, into the eternal fire prepared for the devil and his angels."* (Matt.25:41).

Spirituality, I believe, is not some mystical personal thing that we keep up with daily devotions, but it has to do with *others*. From the greatest commandment and from what Paul taught in 1 Cor.13 and from what John taught in his epistle, the true test of spirituality is love – love of God and love of our neighbors, especially those in need. There is no doubt that we cannot earn our salvation by good works, but this is the inescapable conclusion from Lk.10:25-37 and Matt.25:31-46 : *my salvation/eternal life, has to do with loving others. God's Kingdom is a Kingdom of love and we are not part of His Kingdom if His love does not beat in our hearts and our lives do not exhibit that love.*

Many of us have memorized Eph.2:8-9 *"For it is by grace you have been saved, through faith – and this not from yourselves, it is the gift of God – not by works, so that no one can boast."* But we stop there and ignore verse 10. Yes we are saved not by works, but what are we saved for? Verse 10 says *"For we are God's handiwork, created in Christ Jesus to do good works, which God prepared in advance for us to do."*

Knowing God's Heart

Please understand that I am not trying to get you to go and love the poor so that you can be saved, or to be sure of your salvation. That is not the point. If you think I'm trying to do that, you have misunderstood me. Neither am I trying to persuade or convince you to go and love the poor. Although the statistics (Appendix 1) speak for themselves, the problem is not so much that we are neglecting the poor. The problem is that we don't know God. The apostle John said that if we know God, we would love, because God is love (1 Jn.4:8).

If I know God, I will feel His heart for people, especially the needy. Just as Jesus was naturally attracted to the poor, if we know Him, if we know His heart, we would also be naturally attracted to the poor. Loving the poor would be a natural thing for us if we love God. No one will need to tell us to go and love the poor. People who go and love the poor because someone told them to or because they think it is their Christian duty are no different from people of other faiths or humanitarian people who do that because they think it is the right or virtuous or religious thing to do.

Or that it will save them. John was emphatic that those who do not love, do not really know God, no matter how much they think they know God or claim to belong to Him. See also Jer.22:16 where God Himself declares what it means to know Him.

This is so fundamental and yet so tragically and glaringly absent from church as we know it, that it begs to be repeated in the simplest of terms : If I am truly God's child, I will have His Spirit, and if I have His Spirit, then His love will be moving in me to go and love those in need. This is the inescapable conclusion from John's epistle – if we truly love God, it would be evidenced by our love for others – especially those in need. And if I haven't been doing that, what does it mean? Well it means I don't have God's Spirit in me, and I have a false assumption that I do. No matter how "charismatic" I may be, one day Jesus will say to me, *"I never knew you."* (Matt.7:21-23). It's like what James says in his epistle. True faith will lead to action. No action means no faith. By the way, the "action" that James was talking about is caring for the needy (James 2:14-17). And those who think they have faith but it is not evidenced by action are only deceiving themselves : James 1:22. It also means that I have misunderstood the Gospel.

What does it mean to be in God's Kingdom? God's Kingdom is a Kingdom of love. In God's Kingdom the focus is not our personal salvation. The focus is "others". Jesus showed us what it means to love. Jesus left His world to enter into our world. He was called "Immanuel" : God with us. He said, *"As the Father has sent me, I send you."* (Jn.20:21). He sends us to leave our world and enter into the world of others – especially those in need. To love is to focus on the other person. To love someone is to be concerned for him, to understand what he is going through – his struggles, his problems, his frustrations, his pain, his hopes, his fears, to consider and feel what he is feeling, to be a friend, to listen and to emphatize, to share in his pain, making his story our story, to walk with him and help him out of his situation, to help him discover his full potential, and to help him realize his dreams. Going further, if we follow Jesus, then just as He laid down His life for us, we would also lay down our lives for others. (1Jn.3:16). This is the heart and soul of the Kingdom – loving God and loving our neighbors. I believe this is what it means to be part of the Kingdom.

Is it possible that we can "accept Jesus as our savior", believe that the Bible is true, attend church faithfully for years and years and yet one day stand before the Lord on judgment day and be told that we never really knew Him and were never part of His Kingdom? Please read Appendix 5 where I have addressed these points and about forsaking all, total commitment, discipleship, knowing God, loving our neighbors as ourselves and salvation, and how they are all linked together. And how is it possible to love our neighbors as ourselves? How can we have God's love? I trust you will find the answers to these vital questions by the end of the book.

For small group discussion :

1. What is love?
2. What does it mean to know God? Why would knowing God be evidenced by love?
3. Why does the apostle John make love the acid test for being part of God's Kingdom? (1 Jn.3:14, 16-19, 1 Jn.4:7-8, Jn.17:3)
4. What should we do if we know we do not have God's love?
5. How is it possible that those who do "great things" for God might not actually know God? (Matt.7:21-23)

Chapter 6

Back to Square One

What on earth are we doing here? Every Sunday throughout the world billions of Christians pray "Your Kingdom come, Your will be done, on earth as it is in heaven", but do we know what we are praying?

Heaven or Earth?

As I read on in my Bible, my next surprise was when I came to realize that Jesus did not preach the Gospel of salvation but the Gospel of the Kingdom.

What is the difference between the Gospel of salvation as we know it, and the Gospel of the Kingdom that Jesus preached? The focus of the Gospel of salvation as we know it, is heaven. We want to get everyone to heaven. With heaven as our focus, it is no wonder we are not concerned about what happens on earth. However, the focus of the Gospel of the Kingdom is not heaven, but earth. In the "Lord's Prayer" Jesus taught us to pray, *"Your kingdom come, Your will be done, on earth as it is in heaven"* (Matt.6:10). That tells us that God wants His Kingdom to come and penetrate into every sphere and aspect of life on earth so that He would be Lord of all. Salvation, as essential as that is, is but a part of that Kingdom – the entrance into His Kingdom. God is not only concerned for each person's eternal future but also his life and his relationships on earth. His Kingdom begins here and now. He wants His Kingdom to rule both in the hearts of individuals as well as in every family, community, workplace and nation.

What does that mean, practically? What would it look like if government, education, business, the sciences, the arts, sports, and even entertainment were under God's Kingdom? Before we explore that further, let's ask why God created us in the first place.

Back to Genesis

We know that Jn.3:16 is the solution. But what is the problem? In Appendix 5, I said that we misinterpret and misunderstand the solution (Jn.3:16) when we misunderstand the problem – of what went wrong in the Garden of Eden. In this chapter, we are going to take one step even further back. When we ask what the problem is, we must ask, "What was the original design?" In fact, whenever we want to know what a problem is with anything, we must go back to its original design. Only then can we know what has gone wrong with that thing.

As I re-read the Bible with new eyes, I came to realize that Jesus came to redeem and restore what God had intended from the beginning when He created us. The Gospel of the Kingdom is about getting back to God's original design. From the time of Genesis till now, God has not changed His plans. He still intends His Kingdom to be established on earth. And the end of the story has already been written. God is going to get what He set out to do from the beginning :

> *"The kingdom of the world has become the kingdom of the Lord and of His Messiah, and He will reign forever and ever."* (Rev.11:15)

It was revealed to Daniel that God's Kingdom will come and crush all other earthly kingdoms and it will eventually fill the earth (Dan.2:35, 44). Isaiah prophesied the increase of His government (Isa.9:6-7) and that *"the earth will be full of the knowledge of the LORD as the waters cover the sea"* (Isa.11:9).

Another surprise came when I considered how both Jesus *and the disciples* preached the Gospel of the Kingdom (Lk.9:2,6) *before* Jesus was crucified. The disciples at that time did not know that salvation would come through the death of Jesus. They were disillusioned when Jesus died. We can be quite sure they were not preaching the Gospel of salvation as we know it. So what was the Gospel of the Kingdom that they preached? It was about God's Kingdom coming on earth and the deliverance and blessings they would experience from oppression and suffering. That was the Kingdom they were looking for. Not something in the afterlife, but God's Kingdom *on earth* : Isa.2:1-4, Isa.9:6-7, Isa. 11:1-9, Isa.40:1-5, 9, Isa.52:7-9, Isa.61:1-7, Dan.2:44, Dan.7:13-14, 17-18, 22, 27, Am.9:11-14, Mk.1:14-15, Mk.15:43, Lk.1:30-33, 46-55, 68-79, Lk.2:25-32, 38, and Lk.4:18-19.

No doubt the disciples misinterpreted Old Testament prophecies of the Kingdom by understanding them only in terms of the restoration of the Kingdom to Israel (Acts 1:6). They did not understand that God's plans for His Kingdom on earth were not only for the nation of Israel but are for all peoples. They were also mistaken as to when that would happen (Lk.19:11). And they mistakenly looked at Jesus as a political Messiah who would deliver them from the Romans (Jn.6:15). Though Jesus tried to dispel their mistaken expectations, they did not understand Him (Matt.20:17-21). When Jesus did not fight back but let Himself be arrested and crucified in fulfillment of Isaiah's and Daniel's prophecies (Isa.53, Dan.9:26), they were shattered. Later Jesus explained to them and they became somewhat aware of their mistake (Lk.24:13-27, 44-47, Acts 2:23).

One thing however that Jesus did not correct them on, was what He had first sent them out to preach (Lk.9:2, 6) which He again affirmed just before His ascension (Acts 1:3-8) – His Kingdom has not only a spiritual but also an earthly dimension to it (Matt.5:13-16, Lk.19:11-27, Matt.25:14-46). We are to be engaged with God in the restoration of all things that begun with John the Baptist ushering in the Kingdom (Matt.11:12, Acts3:21, Col.1:15-20, 1 Cor.15:24-25). The first church understood this and lived it out (Acts 2:44-47, Acts 4:32-35) and they eventually overcame their Roman persecutors through their love and courage and turned the Roman empire upside down.

Often charismatics only spiritualize Lk.4:18-19, with no thought about actual physical poverty, suffering, exploitation and oppression. For many years I had been one amongst millions of other charismatics that never gave any thought at all to these things. But the good news that Jesus had for the poor, though it no doubt included the spiritual dimension, was nevertheless intended by Jesus to also refer to physical provision for the poor and freedom from physical slavery, exploitation and oppression on earth : Matt.5:3-10, Lk.6:20-26.

And what is the outcome of Jesus' ministry? Not only demons cast out and people miraculously healed, but the hungry are fed, there is restitution of money wrongly extorted (Zaccheus), the marginalized, nobodies and rejects of society are honored and given priority, while the rich, powerful and connected are "put in their place", hypocrisy is exposed, the wickedness of and oppression by those in authority are denounced, those unfairly accused and treated get justice and dignity (woman caught in adultery), etc. – all very earthly issues.

No wonder it was said in Heb.4:2,6 that the Gospel was preached to the Israelites in the desert. Surely that was not about salvation through the death of Jesus. Rather, it was about returning to God and enjoying the rest that He intended for them – the rest they would have in a land of their own under God's rule, and enjoy the abundance He had for them, if only they had submitted to God's plans for them (Deut.11:8-12, 12:10, Jos.1:13)

Finally, Gal.3:8 confirmed to me that the Gospel's mandate to us is similar to what was given to Abraham – that as all nations would be blessed through him, so they would be blessed through us. As children of Abraham we would be the channels of God's original intention for creating the world. Through us, the world would come to experience the abundant life that was lost when Adam and Eve chose to be independent of God.

Made in the Image of God – the Genesis Mandate

My re-reading of Genesis opened my eyes to other things. When we think of God, we usually think of God as one. We also think of God as a Trinity, but when we think of that, we usually think of that only doctrinally. I did not realize this previously but on re-reading Genesis, I suddenly saw that God (Father, Son and Holy Spirit) is *a community*. So what does it mean to be made in the image of God (Gen.1:26, 5:1-2)? Well if we were made to be like Him, then God intended us not just to be individuals but to also be community. We were made to be community. *That's why loving our neighbors as ourselves is part of the greatest commandment, and that has to permeate everything we do as ministry.*

Next, if God is our creator, and we were created to be like Him, then we were also created to be creative. God is also a God of order and structure. Though equal with the Father, the Son submits to the Father. And think of order and structure, vision, organization, planning, step by step progression, and development, within a time frame, in the creation – "On the first day God created .. on the second day God created .." And think of order in the universe. So we were created to be people of vision and have order and structure – in family and other relationships, in thinking, in communication, in work and in everything else in life. Not disorder and chaos, or lack of planning or no planning at all, that we see in so many cultures and nations where the minds of the people are still deeply rooted in false religions – a reflection of the chaotic spiritual world they believe in.

In Genesis, God also put man in the Garden of Eden to work it and take care of it (Gen.2:15). This was before the fall. Work is not a curse (as some teach) but rather a blessing to be enjoyed. Like our creator, when we work and produce something, we can stand back and look at it and feel a sense of satisfaction and say "It is good". When we put our heart, soul, mind and strength into our work using the talents He has given to us, and not just in the big things, but in even something as simple as washing dishes, or sweeping the floor, or arranging the shelves, and we produce something of order and beauty, and we take delight in it, we are fulfilling a part of the image of God that we were created to be. That would be part of the worship (giving worth) to God for creating us.

Imagine if we had this attitude towards our work. Every morning when we wake up, we would look forward to a brand new day to work and rejoice in our work. Imagine how productive we would be and we might even influence and infect others with this same spirit towards work and life and our Creator. Isn't that what it means to be salt and light?"

God also told man to be fruitful and multiply. So we were created to work creatively with what God has given us and to be productive. God gives us seeds to work with, but this is not necessarily limited to physical seeds that produce plants that produce fruits, but also seeds as creative ideas that can germinate in our minds to produce things in the sciences (engineering, architecture, transport and travel, medicine and heath, etc) and the arts (music, writing, painting, design, drama and plays, etc) of efficiency and beauty and that blesses the nations.

The oft quoted example is of George Washington Carver, the son of a black American slave, who discovered more than 300 uses to the groundnut that helped diversify from the failing cotton industry at that time and possibly saved tens of thousands of lives. I also read some time ago of someone who walked into a slum one day. He saw the terrible consequences to lack of sanitation and clean water, and he came up with a creative idea to get sponsorship of banks and multinational companies with big name brands, to provide toilets and clean water for slums around the world. He and his friends have over the years saved tens of thousands of lives. And lately someone came up with the idea of solar light bulbs for slums using only a plastic water bottle filled with water and a bit of bleach. Someone else is recycling garbage to turn it into bricks.

And we are to be a community of love – serving one another and sharing both our resources and the fruits of our labor, and if we would do that then there would be no poor among us (Deut.15:4-11). And when we fulfill the potential that God created us to be, we glorify Him by showing forth and reflecting the glory of our Maker. (See what William Carey did in Appendix 2. See also my Ghana story in Appendix 6).

I need to keep this book short and concise, but one thing in particular I must highlight and elaborate a little is about serving one another. Here is something the Lord opened my eyes to one day. What do we normally think of when we sing of the greatness of God? Perhaps many of us would imagine God on His throne with the rainbow and angels and worship and glory surrounding Him. Or we might think of the mountains and stars and the amazing greatness of His creation. One day, I was worshipping and singing, "How great is our God .." Instead of thinking of the glory and power of God, I had a picture of Jesus kneeling down washing the feet of his disciples. Imagine the Almighty God of the universe doing that. I broke down and cried, "Oh God, You are great. Who is like You?"

Later the Lord drew my attention to Isa.57:15 and Isa.66:1-2. Imagine you are looking for a home. Where and with whom would you choose to live? God seeks to be with the lowly and dwell in the heart of one who is lowly, broken and contrite and who trembles at His word. That describes a servant. Why would God who lives in a high and lofty place, choose to be with a lowly servant? I believe it is because He feels most at home with someone who is like Him. Jesus became a servant because He is a servant at heart. To become more and more like Him is to become more and more of a servant to others. And to be created in His image means that we are to be a community of people who serve one another.

If it can be said that there are certain core truths in the Bible, I believe one of them must be that God is love and that we were made to be like Him, meaning we were made to love. We become most like Him, most alive, and find our greatest joy and fulfilment when we love – when we feel for others, when we give, and when we bring joy to others and serve others. Not when we are immersed in ourselves, and accumulate, and hoard and serve ourselves. This is a paradox but the more we seek fulfilment for ourselves, the further we will be from finding it, because the further we will be from what we were created to be. But the more we turn our gaze away from ourselves and love and give and serve, the closer we will be to what we were created to be, and the more we will experience fulfilment.

Back to the main point about being made in God's image and understanding that as the defining be all and end all of life. Imagine such communities and imagine all this working out in every sphere of life on earth, along with the spiritual dimension – constant communion with God, knowing and obeying the Word, becoming more and more like Christ, worship and prayer, healing and miracles, and the operation and manifestation of the prophetic and other spiritual gifts, all under the Lordship of Christ. Would that not be a picture of the Kingdom on earth? And what would the role of the church – the people of God – be, in all this?

Paul said that we, the redeemed of the Lord, are the secret that God has kept in ages past to be revealed in the end times, that through the church, God's eternal purpose would be realized (Eph.3:7-11). In other words we were meant to be the agents of God's Kingdom coming to earth (Matt.16:18-19). Binding and loosing involves a far greater dimension than what most Pentecostals and Charismatics understand and focus on. That's why we are to pray, *"Your kingdom come, Your will be done, on earth as it is in heaven"* (Matt.6:10). By the way, have you ever wondered why it is necessary for us to pray? Can God not act without us praying? And why does God want us to be His co-workers? I have addressed this in Appendix 9.

What does it mean to be agents of God's Kingdom advance? I believe it means being salt and light, influencing towards change, discipling nations not just in the spiritual things but in everything including the Genesis mandate towards God's original purpose for His Kingdom to reign on earth. That would include transforming cultures to God's ways – to God's Kingdom culture. When I say "culture" I do not mean change in the way people dress or what they eat or other external inconsequential social customs. I am referring more to worldview, belief and values that make up the deeper core of cultures. Please see the works and publications of Darrow Miller and Disciple Nations Alliance and the other "heavier" books in the Bibliography. For easy reading I have written an overview which you can find here:

https://acts1322issachar.wordpress.com/worldview-and-the-kingdom-of-god/

God expected this from the nation of Israel, but when they failed in their mission, Jesus said the Kingdom was taken away from them and given to a people who would bear fruit (Matt.21:43). Who do you think that is? Yes, it is we, the church of Jesus Christ.

When I came to realize this, I looked back at what we have become as the church and I asked myself, "Is that how we see ourselves as the church? Do we realize that God is in the process of restoring everything back to His original design? Do we realize that God's Kingdom has come to invade Satan's kingdom and we are the agents of the Kingdom through whom God will establish His Kingdom on earth?"

For small group discussion :

1. Prior to reading this chapter, has it ever struck you that Jesus and the disciples preached quite a different Gospel to the salvation Gospel that most Christians know? What do you think of that now?
2. What was your understanding of *"Your kingdom come, Your will be done, on earth as it is in heaven"*? How would you pray that now?
3. What is the connection between the Gospel of the Kingdom and why God created us?
4. How can work become a very spiritual and fulfilling thing and for someone to become part of God's Kingdom invasion without him being in "full-time ministry"?

Chapter 7

Let's Step Out of the Box for a Second

"If you want to know what water is, don't ask the fish"

(an old Chinese proverb)

What is Church?

Suppose I were to ask you to close your eyes and I would give you a word, let's say "table", what would you see in your mind's eye? Each of us would imagine different sizes, types and colors of tables. Now let's try another word, "church" – what do you see?

I have carried out this little test/exercise in many churches and Christian gatherings I have spoken in all over the world. The results are consistent. Between 60-70% of people saw a building. About 30-40% of people saw people. Most of those who saw a building saw a steeple with a cross on it. For those who saw people, I would say to them, "Before you congratulate yourselves that you have the right answer – that church is not a building but people, I have to ask you this – in what you saw in your mind's eye, what were the people doing?" Again the results have been consistent. All of the people who saw people, saw them in a meeting – either in a church service or Bible study or cell group whether in a church building or some other building or even on the beach, but still in a meeting.

So there is a meeting on Wednesday we call the mid week prayer meeting or Bible study, then there is another meeting on Saturday we call the youth meeting, and another one we call the children's meeting, and another one we call the women's meeting, and on Sunday, the most important meeting of all, we call the Sunday service. Meeting, meeting, meeting, meeting and meeting! Imagine, this is how we look at ourselves today – we are either a building or a meeting. Is it any wonder the world thinks we are irrelevant? When the world is trying to deal with HIV, terrorism, racism, suicides, youth and gang violence, corruption, trafficking, global economic crisis, do they come and consult with the church? Why not?

Sadly, today, church as we know it, is just an institution that holds regular meetings or gatherings where the focus is only on the spiritual and our focus is to get away from this world that is perishing and get as many people as possible to heaven. How can we be agents of the Kingdom when we do not even realize we are meant to be agents of the Kingdom? Not only do we not have a vision of the Kingdom, we have withdrawn from the world in the belief that God has no plans for this world. In fact the general belief of the church is that God is going to destroy this world and start all over again and create a new heaven and a new earth. So the reasoning is, why try to change this world if it is doomed to perish?

Well, if that is the right way of looking at it, let's take it to its logical conclusion. Does that mean we stop eating, traveling, going to school, to university, to work, to improve things around us? Do we, or do we not, have a role in how things function on this earth?

Most Christians have never thought much about this, but if pressed, most would think that perhaps what the Bible requires us to be is to be good citizens so that we would be good witnesses – again the focus is on getting people saved from this world. So we do just the minimum – just be harmless citizens doing our little bit here and there, but largely retreating into our church meetings to prepare for heaven? Just turn a blind eye to all the problems happening around us and pretend they don't exist? And just pray God will shield and protect us from the evil of this world? And wait for God to come and destroy this world and start all over again? And while we wait, the belief is that some individuals have a calling to go into the "full-time" ministry and a few others ("thankfully not me!") are called to the mission field to save souls and plant churches?

Is that not how we think and behave? Just one example : Our schools are bad, so what do we do? Instead of joining the PTA and participating to effect change, and influencing the school to adopt Biblical values of excellence, and training our children to shine in school, we pull our children out of school and start home-schooling them or start Christian schools. How can we be salt and light in this world if we keep doing this? (I do accept however that there may be extreme cases where homeschooling and Christian schools may be needed). How can we be salt and light if we see ourselves as only a meeting in a building? What does it mean to be salt and light (Matt.5:13-16)? In today's language, I think it would mean to be relevant and visible. And to be an influence and an agent of change. Jesus said no one lights a lamp and puts it under a bed. And if salt has lost its savor, it is good for nothing and fit to be thrown out.

What about issues of justice and righteousness in this world? What about the racism, hatred, violence and corruption and compromise that is eating away the fabric of society? Is God no longer concerned about these? Does He have no role for us for justice and righteousness to prevail in this world? I often hear Christians saying not to get involved in politics because politics is a dirty business. What happens when all the Christians withdraw from involvement with public life? When we withdraw from the world, we let the world define what science is, what art is, what music is, what business, economics and government is, and determine how this world should function. Lately, even marriage and family are being re-defined by the world.

How about creation care? The Bible tells us that, *"The earth is the Lord's, and everything in it."* (Ps.24:1). When God created man He entrusted to man the responsibility to care for this earth (see Gen.1:28, 2:15,19). Has God ever changed His mind about that? Is God no longer concerned about His creation? I don't believe so. If God has changed His mind and He no longer holds us responsible for creation care, why is it clearly stated in Rev.11:18 that He will destroy those who destroy the earth? Yes no doubt the end has already been written – God is going to destroy everything by fire and bring in a new heaven and new earth, but that is His prerogative and He alone decides the time for that. Until such time, we still bear the responsibility He has entrusted us with, to steward and care for His creation.

Environmental issues today are no longer just about preserving endangered species, conserving resources and stewardship of the natural beauty of the earth. It has also to do with justice for the poor. Global warming and deforestation for example cause floods that devastate the lives of the poor who have nowhere to live except in the most flood-prone areas. Numerous resources available on the internet show how global climate change and other environmental issues have caused the deaths of hundreds of thousands each year and affected the lives of more than a billion poor people. We may not give much thought to it but in fact every moral choice we make in the way we go about our work and our lives for profit and gain has social, economic and physical consequences for the defenseless and vulnerable poor somewhere down the road.

Will we be able to change this world before Jesus comes again? The answer is definitely "No". The Bible is clear enough how a new heaven and new earth will be inaugurated only when Jesus comes again. But does the fact that we will not be able to transform this world in every area negate Jesus' own call for us to be salt and light? What did Jesus mean when He said, *"Occupy till I come."* (Lk.19:13 KJV)? What if William Wilberforce for example had sat back and thought it pointless to try and do anything about slavery, because Jesus would someday come and wipe everything out and start all over again anyway, would slavery have been eradicated?

What if Abraham Lincoln, Martin Luther King Jr., Ghandi, Nelson Mandela, Mother Theresa and others throughout history, who worked hard and fought for civil liberties, respect for human dignity and clean government and emancipation of the poor, had sat back and thought it pointless to try and do anything because God is going to come and destroy everything one day? What if countless others like Issac Newton, Edison, and Marconi who blessed us with modern inventions and changed life on earth, had sat back and thought the same? Can you see how absurd that kind of thinking is?

OK, let's say, just for argument's sake, we agree with those who say that God has not called us to be agents of change or agents of His Kingdom transformation to come on the earth, or that God's Kingdom involves only the spiritual – that it does not involve work, food, sanitation, garbage disposal, clean efficient government, sciences and arts, etc., and we reason that God is going to come and destroy everything one day and start all over again anyway, so why try to change anything now. Let's say we agree with all that. WHAT ABOUT THE COMMAND TO LOVE OUR NEIGHBORS AS OURSELVES?

Where do we draw the line when loving our neighbors would not involve going further to effect change in our world? How is that possible in the complex inter-twined systems in the world we live in today where everything affects and has an impact on everything else? Even if we could withdraw and hide ourselves from this world, which is impossible, how would we be loving our neighbors if we withdrew from the world and just turned a blind eye to the rot that is going on and that is affecting our neighbors? Isn't that what the priest and Levite did? They just conveniently passed by on the other side (Lk.10:31-32).

Why Did the Priest and Levite Pass By on the Other Side?

In Myanmar, there was a man who lived at a bus stop with his wife and 2 children for two months, totally destitute, sick and hungry. Nearby was a Bible college with 200 students. Every day, those 200 students and their lecturers would pass by that bus stop, but none of them reached out to help the man. After two months, he eventually wasted away and died. Why did no one stop to help them?

I have been asking that question in many churches : "Why did the priest and the Levite pass by on the other side?" One pastor in India gave an interesting answer. He said, "Because the TV camera crew was not there!" Others have answered, "Because they were busy", "Because it was not convenient to stop and help", and "Because they were late for church!" How true! The man who was beaten up was going from Jerusalem to Jericho. The priest and Levite passed by on the other side. Although we cannot be certain, in all likelihood, they were traveling from Jericho to Jerusalem. Where else would a priest and Levite be heading? They were going to the temple – "Church" as it was for them.

Aren't we the same? We are so busy with Church that we have no time to be concerned about the needs of the poor. The best answers came from a group of Sunday school kids from a slum. One little boy said, "I know Uncle, it's because the priest and Levite did not want to get dirty." Another little girl said, "I know Uncle, they thought that someone else would help the man." Perhaps they were speaking from their own experiences. But their answers are really so telling. We don't want to get dirty, and we always think someone else will do it.

We can postulate this or that, as to why they passed by on the other side, but basically, the church today is no different from the priest and Levite. We believe it is not our responsibility. We have to be focused on the more spiritual things. Isn't it because the church has misunderstood the Gospel that 200 Bible school students and their lecturers could pass by everyday without helping the family living at the bus stop? And 96% of all money given stays in the church? (see Appendix 1)

Church or Kingdom?

The Bible talks about three kingdoms – God's Kingdom, Satan's kingdom, and the kingdoms of the world. Every kingdom has three things : the King, his subjects and his domain – the realm over which the King reigns. Where is the domain of God's kingdom? It is in heaven. That's why Jesus called it the kingdom of heaven. But God wants His kingdom not only in heaven but on earth (Matt.6:10). God gave Adam dominion over the earth (Gen.1:26, Ps.115:16). What did he do with it? When Adam listened to Satan instead of God, he gave up his dominion to Satan (Lk.4:5-6, Rom.6:16) and Satan became the prince of this world. But Psalm 24:1 says that the earth is the Lord's and everything in it. God has never given up ownership of the earth and all that is in it. Jesus came not only to save us from hell but to invade Satan's kingdom (Matt.11:12) and drive Satan out (Jn.12:31). After His resurrection, Jesus proclaimed that He had won back all authority in heaven and on earth and He sent us, the church, out to disciple nations (Matt.28:18-20) – that means to bring all nations back to obedience (Rom.16:26).

The end has already been written – God's Kingdom will keep advancing until Satan's rule and control over every sphere and area of life on earth is totally destroyed. In Daniel's vision he saw the Kingdom of God as a rock that struck and destroyed all other kingdoms and it grew into a huge mountain that filled the whole earth (Dan2:35, 44-45). Isaiah prophesied the *increase* of His government (Isa.9:6-7) and John saw that one day all the kingdoms of the world will become the Kingdom of God (Rev.11:15). The earth will be filled with the knowledge of the glory of the Lord as the waters cover the sea (Isa.11:9, Hab.2:14). This is a description of what will happen on earth, not in heaven. In Col.1:15-20 Paul said that all things were created by Him and for Him, and through Jesus, God will reconcile to Himself all things, whether things on earth or things in heaven, so that in everything He would be Lord over all.

In 1 Cor.15:24-28, Paul said that Jesus will destroy all dominion, authority and power, and everything will be brought into subjection under His Lordship and then He will hand the Kingdom over to His Father : *"For he must reign until he has put all his enemies under his feet."* That means that Jesus is already reigning (Matt.28:18 confirms that) and the process of taking back dominion is already underway. A Greek word study reveals the principalities and powers that Paul talked about (Eph.6:12, Rom.8:37, Col.1:16, Col.2:15, Eph.3:10, see also Mk.5:9-10, Dan.10:13,20) to be spiritual or angelic beings that rule over geographical/territorial regions, and over jurisdictions, systems and domains, not just individuals. Wherever they are cast out and displaced by the Holy Spirit, there the Kingdom of God has come (Matt.12:28). Jesus will return one day to complete what He started, but we are to already be part of that restoration (Acts.3:21) that has begun, and we are to be part of that Kingdom advance *now* (Matt.16:18-19). Notice that Jesus said "now" twice in Jn.12:31. What then is the church in relation to the Kingdom? The church are people who are subjects of the King. They are the community of the King, and the agents of God's Kingdom advance!

In the light of God's Kingdom mandate, what do we see of church today? Do we see churches today gripped by a vision of the Kingdom (notice I said "Kingdom"; not "Church") ousting the forces of darkness and taking back every domain on earth? Sadly that is not what I see. Instead, as I travel the world, this is what I see of churches. Imagine a group of people at a car showroom being introduced to the latest car in the market. They spend hours examining every inch of the car and spend even more hours absorbed in learning all about the power and efficiency of the engine and in its technically advanced suspension system. Then they get into the car, start up the engine and switch on the air-conditioning and spend hours enjoying its sound system and plush interior and they turn their attention to all the latest computerized gadgets in the car. They are so absorbed in the car itself that they forget what the car is for. The next day, and every week for the next 10 years they come and do the same. They do everything else except drive the car to some place. That may sound absurd, but that might not be too far off as a picture of the Church that is so focused on the Church itself and has lost the purpose of what the church is for.

Here's another thing that for many years as a leader in Church and in "full-time" ministry, I did not realize. It struck me only after my re-reading of the Bible that Jesus talked about church only twice (Matt.16:18, 18:17), and He never even explained what He meant by "church". All the time He kept talking about the Kingdom of God. But we keep talking about church. Imagine if you were Jesus and you were about to leave your apostles and go back to heaven. They are going to be the pioneers of a new worldwide movement called "church". Wouldn't you prepare your apostles in how to run church? Yet isn't it really amazing that Jesus never gave a seminar or training to His apostles about what church is or should be, nor how church should be run. Could it be that we have really got it wrong and focused on the wrong thing – on "Church" instead of "God's Kingdom" and we have made it into an institution?

Isn't it because the Church is so focused on Church rather than on God's Kingdom, that there are now more than 41,000 denominations in the world? Isn't that because we keep thinking of the Church as an institution and we keep trying to re-define what church is? And each denomination thinks theirs is the right one? Otherwise why have yet another denomination? Incidentally that tells me that there are at least 41,000 definitions of "church" today! If unbelievers were aware of this, I can imagine what they would say : "You guys must be crazy. You have 41,000 divisions and you want us to join you?"

In chapter 6 we looked at order and structure. There is no doubt that as the people of God we are to be organized. But being organized does not mean it should change our nature from being people to being a corporate entity. God did not intend the church to be an institution or corporation to conduct services or do evangelism or missions or ministry. *The command to disciple nations and to love and serve is to the church as the people of God, not to the church as an institution or corporation.* But because we think of the Church as the institution or organ to do ministry, isn't that why in an average church less than 10% of its members are engaged in ministry, while 90% are just passive spectators?

If we confine "ministry" to the "spiritual", and therefore only "full-time" ministry workers do the work of the ministry, we will never be able to fulfill God's mandate in Matt.28 to disciple nations. The rate at which we are raising up "full-time" ministry workers is being far exceeded by the natural birth rate of nations by millions of times.

If we truly understand the Kingdom, "ministry" will not only be preaching, teaching, prayer, Bible study, etc. but we would see ourselves as agents of reconciliation and transformation in every aspect of life. Our role would not be to try and get people to heaven, but to live out Kingdom values and to be God's agent for His Kingdom to come into every sphere of life. We would bring Biblical truth and love, and His Lordship to every work place and community, and the skills and natural talents of every Christian would be ministry. It is by this that nations will be discipled and His Kingdom can come. However, instead of a vision for Kingdom advance, sadly the church today is self-focused and self-absorbed in a vision of church growth.

Church Growth	v.	Kingdom Advance
"Bring them in"		"Send them out"
Navel Gazing : "How Are We Doing?		Outward Vision : "Lift up your eyes and look at the fields ..
Congregation, Membership, and Building		Engaging People and Communities
Order and Program		Creative Ventures
Guarding Territory		Taking Territory
Growth and Succession		Multiplication

What is the difference between church growth and Kingdom advance? I believe that it might be comparable with the difference between guys who go to the gym to build muscles, and guys who go and dig a well for a poor village. In the gym you can see guys building muscles for no other reason than to have bigger and bigger muscles. If someone were to ask those guys in the gym what they did with all their bulging muscles, they probably would not be able to answer you. But Kingdom advance would be like the guys who get out there and dig wells and while they are doing it they naturally build some muscles also.

As we look at the immense social needs around us, is any of the church growth today impacting the world in any way? Is this focus on "church growth" of having bigger and bigger congregations and bigger and bigger buildings even a Biblical idea? Is that what Jesus did, and taught His disciples to do? Are any of us in any doubt that when the first church grew in size, it was God Himself who allowed persecution to scatter them from Jerusalem so that they would not get self-focused but get out there to advance His Kingdom (Acts 8:1,4, Acts 11:19-21)?

From the "Church" perspective, let's get people into Church and into heaven. But from the Kingdom perspective, our role should not be to try and get people to heaven, but to live out Kingdom values and be God's agent for His Kingdom to come into every sphere of life. Instead of withdrawing from this world, and being absorbed with ourselves, we would be asking the Lord how we can become agents of His Kingdom transformation in this world. We would be penetrating into the world and affecting the world – business, education, art, entertainment, sports, engineering, science, technology, civil administration, government, social concerns, family, environment, etc. – with Biblical values. Jesus told us to occupy till He comes (Lk.19:13 KJV), not run and hide till He comes.

How did we become the way we are now? I think it has a lot to do with church history. I owe it to Ben Wong who first pointed this out to me. It all began with how the pagan emperor Constantine "became a Christian" in order to solidify his political power. As part of his strategy he institutionalized the church. And he commissioned the building of huge cathedrals and compelled the masses (that's where the word "mass" for Sunday service came from) into "Church". Did you know that before Constantine, for the first 300 years, there was no church building, but Christians gathered in houses among neighborhoods where the people live? Church was community. They shared whatever they had with people in need in their communities. That's how the church, meaning house churches, multiplied rapidly (Acts 2:44-47, 4:32-35)

All that ended when Christianity became institutionalized. How sad that up till today, we continue to follow that unbiblical model or structure that Constantine forced onto the church. Unfortunately in the Reformation, Martin Luther did not think it important to change the structure. But the wrong structure can kill the substance. The institutional church in Europe has died. The institutional church in the US is dying. What will become of the institutional church in Asia and Africa?

We Have Been Deceived

Church history is what we study and observe on the surface. Underneath it, the devil has been at work blinding and deceiving not only the nations from the truth of salvation, but blinding and deceiving the church from God's purposes for us and the role He has for us in this world. In as much as salvation has been hidden from unbelievers, the Kingdom has been hidden from the church. At the very core, it is a battle between truth and lies. Truth leads to life. False ideas or lies lead to death. God is for life. He is the giver of life. The devil steals, kills and destroys all that God intends for us (abundant life) by telling us lies (Jn.8:44, 10:10). And we have been kept for centuries from seeing what church was meant to be and seeing ourselves as the agents of the Kingdom. The consequences for this has been devastating. Think of the millions and millions of lives, families and communities that could have been saved and transformed had we understood the Gospel of the Kingdom. Even as I go around sharing this, I find that while there are people awakening to this, many still have such difficulty appreciating this or are even resistant to it. They simply cannot comprehend "church" to be anything other than what it has always been.

Ravi Zacharias in his book "Deliver Us from Evil" has a section entitled "Imperiled by Immersion" that describes this phenomenon so well. He tells of an old Chinese proverb that says that if you want to know what water is, don't ask the fish. The fish is so immersed in the monotony and single vision of a watery existence that to the fish no other existence is possible. Hence it can conceive of nothing else by which to measure its own existence nor is it capable of evaluating the water it is in. Similarly, we can be so immersed in a culture that we can, not only become so desensitized to what someone of another culture looking at our culture may find to be strange or aberrant or hilarious or even repulsive, but we can become incapacitated from being able to recognize it even when someone takes pains to point it out and explain it to us.

He put it so well in his book : "Sometimes a culture can so imperceptibly absorb and transmit ideas into its consciousness that it is hard for those within it to be objective about the propriety of its practices when measured against a counter-perspective. In other words, if we want to know what America is like, the surest way to gain that understanding may not be to ask one who has been culturally American all his or her life." In my years of travels I have found this to be so true. If you visit another nation or culture, you will see things about that nation or culture that the people there cannot see about themselves. In the same way, if they were to visit your nation or culture, they will also see things about your nation or culture that you probably cannot see about yourselves.

Ravi Zacharias was talking about being so immersed in our cultures that we are blind to what it is and what it has done to us. He was speaking more of ethnic cultures and present day modern and post-modern culture. But isn't this also so true of our present day Christian Church culture? Aren't we so immersed in "Church" as we have always known it to be, that we can't see ourselves and what we have become? There is another Chinese proverb which says, "When you are on the mountain, you cannot see the mountain." To see what the mountain looks like, we have to come down from the mountain, and look at it from a distance away. When I once quoted this proverb in a seminar I conducted for some church leaders, one of the participants laughed and said, "We were all born on the mountain and we never came down the mountain!"

Church as we know it has accepted church as we know it as normal to such an extent that most people in church cannot imagine "Church" to be anything else. Though there are many who politely nod in agreement with what I and others are sharing about this, yet most take the path of least resistance and continue to perpetuate this state of denial. Jesus said, *"Those who have drunk the old wine, don't want the new. They will say the old is better."* (Lk.5:39). The amazing thing is that unbelievers can see what the church has become. They are not "in the water" or not "on the mountain" with us. Well not all of what they think about the church is true, but they can certainly see how irrelevant the church has become. Lately, there were a lot of articles in the media of a nation highlighting the glitz and glamour of mega-churches in that nation written with a negative slant. Instead of getting defensive about that, why not ask ourselves how much we have become like the world? Jesus said we are in the world but not of the world. But look at what we have become – we are not in the world (because we have withdrawn ourselves from the world) but we are of the world (worldly)! This is not just about mega-churches. It is about church as we know it around the world.

What would church look like if we were what God meant us to be? Obviously I'm not talking about shifting the furniture around or adding a "serve the poor" department, or adding more social concern activity, to "Church". It has to do more with our identity and a re-visioning of "church" than simply re-structuring how we "do" church. For example, how can we make sense of the question, "What time does church start?" or "Where is your church?" or the expression, "go to church" if *we* are the church? I am tempted to add another appendix on the subject of church but I think I shall not lest I might be interpreted as attempting to come out with a description for the 41,001st denomination! ☺

I don't claim a special hotline to heaven, but as I seek the Lord, my current understanding is that if we keep focusing on "Church", then the Kingdom will not advance (Well, actually the Kingdom will still advance but without us – Jesus said the Kingdom is forcefully advancing (Matt.11:12) – and God will get others. God invites us to partner with Him in His Kingdom advance, but Jesus also said that He doesn't need us. He can make children of Abraham out of stones. There are many nameless and faceless people out there that are not operating under the umbrella of any institution who are loving and living out God's Kingdom). But if we would focus on the Kingdom instead, as Jesus intended us to, then not only would the Kingdom advance, but church (as God meant it to be) would naturally happen.

For small group discussion :

1. What is your understanding of "church"? How does "Imperiled by Immersion" apply to church as we know it?
2. The first church was a community (Acts 2:42-47, 4:32-35). How do you think the church today could become community again?
3. The author talked about living out Kingdom values and becoming God's agent for His Kingdom to come into every sphere of life. What role do you see for yourself as an agent of God's Kingdom in this world?
4. When we read Revelation, we know that the world is going to get worse and worse and further and further away from God. If God Himself is going to destroy everything on earth (2 Pet.3:10-12), why then is there a need for us to continue to steward it? And bring change and transformation in this world?
5. Try to re-imagine what church would be if it were not only a spiritual gathering but also an agent of God's Kingdom transformation in this world.
6. What are 3 areas in which you will work with the Lord to share His love and abundant life with the communities around you?

Chapter 8

Recapturing a Vision of the Kingdom

"The creation waits in eager expectation for the children of God to be revealed" (Rom.8:19) .. "that through the church, the manifold wisdom of God should be made known to the rulers and authorities in the heavenly realms .." (Eph.3:10-11)

Church as People and as Agents of the Kingdom

It goes without saying, but for the avoidance of any doubt, please understand that I am not setting aside the need for salvation. By "Kingdom" I mean it to include salvation. In fact salvation is the entrance into the Kingdom. Of course we desire that people will come into the Kingdom and we would pray for them and share with them the message of salvation (not only salvation from, but salvation to as well), but does the Kingdom coming into our workplace have to begin with everyone being saved first? In our workplace, can we not work with excellence, utilizing the gifts and talents God has given us to joyfully serve the Lord and man, and bring the values and atmosphere of the Kingdom into the workplace and influence others to adopt the same attitude and excellence too? Is that not part of what it means to disciple nations to God's Kingdom truth and culture? Is that also not what it means to be salt and light and to glorify God by reflecting His character?

Is there anything in the Bible that tells us that we cannot influence and affect people with Kingdom values without getting them saved first? What if through our influence others adopt values and practices of excellence as well, and the business not only does well, but produces excellent products and services that serve the public, and co-workers become more patient and kind and forgiving and their families are blessed as a result? And if we are in the health service, because of this change, lives are saved? And in other areas, trains don't crash, fake medicines are not sold, garbage is properly disposed of, universities produce graduates that are more caring and responsible, not just smarter at making money and living selfish lives, governments don't become legalized crime syndicates, employers are fair to their employees, food businesses do not compromise on hygiene, etc. Isn't that what it means to be salt and light?

In 2000, after more than 3500 church buildings had been burned down in Indonesia, I was invited to be part of a conference of more than 400 leaders from all over Indonesia that met to discuss what went wrong and to talk about transformation. I gave a message on the role of the church as agents of God's Kingdom transformation. After I finished, the person who chaired the meeting said to everyone present, "If we had not built all those church buildings and instead we had used the money to feed the poor, maybe they would not have been so angry with us, and there would have been no church buildings to burn down." How true. But has the church in Indonesia learned? I don't think so. Lately there are even more and bigger church buildings springing up everywhere, which hardly any poor ever enter. Young people in Indonesia are telling me that they want to reach out to street children around them, but their church leaders are not interested. They want them instead to be more involved with church programs within their church buildings.

If you are reading this and you are in Indonesia, India, Pakistan, Myanmar, Cairo, or anywhere in Africa, and you are surrounded by slums and poor rural communities, how can you continue with "Church" and ignore what's going on around you? I'm sorry I don't mean to be judgmental, and you may be the exception, but that is what I see of "Church" in all these nations. Almost all the pastors and leaders whom I have interacted with face to face in the nations I have been teaching admit that none of their churches, nor other churches in their nation, put the poor as priority. They also admitted to me that they never had an understanding of the need to serve the poor as part of the Gospel, much less bring transformation to their communities. They confessed that this teaching is not only totally new to them but that it has turned their understanding of the Gospel and of church upside down.

If you are living in any of these places, imagine if you and your Christian friends go and engage with the poor and with people in need around you, and become the catalysts for the transformation of communities around you, wouldn't that be something? I am encouraging you and your friends to do it as individuals. Not going as representatives of an institution that has come to be known as "Church" – please see Appendix 8.

For example, I know some people in Indonesia helping prostitutes to find alternative work so that they can feed their families. And some youth in Jakarta who go and help look after the kids of single mothers and widows in the slums while these women go out the whole day washing clothes from house to house. And someone in Cambodia who has an extra room in their home just to take in those dying of AIDS, to give him or her a loving and clean and decent place to die, instead of dying in the streets.

Other examples : I have a friend in Malaysia who is working among a certain people group where the people are often in debt. He is successfully teaching some families to get out of debt, and they in turn are teaching others to do the same. Another friend in Bangkok is caring for refugees that have no legal status or income. Another friend in Myanmar picks up babies abandoned at garbage dumps. My very good friend Peter Dias in India was instrumental in starting a hotline/online portal to trace missing kids (just one among other things he's initiated). Nothing fanciful, nothing big. And they didn't start an NGO and raise funds either. Just one life or family at a time. Isn't that what it means to be church? Why do you have to wait for your church leaders to organize anything or tell you what to do? And love has to be personal. No one can feel the love of a Church (institution) or NGO. I have addressed this in Appendix 8.

And what if God has gifted you with more education, more abilities and opportunities? One Christian businessman in India started a restaurant just to provide work for the poor. He trained them to do it well and then turned the whole business completely over to them. He does not get even 1 Rupee of the profits. He does not need it. He has other businesses that give him more than enough income for him and his family to live on. He counts it a joy to be able to enable others, especially the poor, to succeed, and not only succeed but also to pass on the vision to them to enable others to do so. Now isn't that a wonderful example of a Kingdom community?

And how about those of us living in more developed nations? Are there no lonely people around us? People whose lives are wrecked by divorce and broken relationships? Or those who are dying of cancer or AIDS? Or seeking out those who are burdened with children with special needs? Or single mothers? Or how about partnering with our brothers and sisters in less developed nations to love the poor around them? I know several people in Singapore who partner with church planters and community workers in poor nations, to help them start small businesses, who then go on to help others in their community do the same.

Please understand that I am certainly not just advocating transformation per se. Our call is not just to make this world a better world. Neither are we to be just need-driven or to bring transformation without the Kingdom or the King. The Kingdom does not advance just by good works and professionally managed social projects. God's Kingdom is here to invade and overthrow Satan's kingdom (Matt.11:12, 12:28, Jn.12:31, Eph.6:12, 2 Cor.10:3-5). Not only is there a spiritual battle involved, we must remember that that which is born of the flesh is flesh and that which is born of the spirit is spirit (Jn.3:6). Flesh and blood cannot do the work of the Kingdom. Unless we are in tune with the Spirit's leading (Jn.5:19, Jn.20:21, Rom.8:14) and allow the power of the Holy Spirit to work in and through us to be instruments of His Kingdom advance (Eph.1:19, 3:20), we will not be working as co-laborers with the Lord (1 Cor.3:6-9). We would be just doing our own thing (Jn.15:5-6, 1 Cor.3:10-15). I hope however that those who focus only on evangelism, signs and wonders and spiritual warfare will see from what I am advocating in this book that the work of the Holy Spirit in bringing about the Kingdom of God on earth is not only in the spiritual dimension.

The Kingdom of God is like …

At this point, perhaps like I did, you might be asking, "So what exactly is the Gospel?" Or "What exactly is the Kingdom?" Or "What exactly is the church?" Some people like definitions. Others like formula. Still others like clear points 1,2,3 .. However through my re-reading of the Gospels over and over again I noticed that Jesus did not define the Gospel, nor the church, nor the Kingdom. He always said, *"The kingdom of God is like ..."* Both the expert in the law (Lk.10:25) and the rich young ruler (Lk.18:18) asked the same identical question, *"What must I do to inherit eternal life?"*, yet Jesus' answer or response to them was not the same. What was similar though was this – it had to do with loving others in need. And Jesus did not give a comprehensive definition of eternal life or salvation but addressed the issues of their heart. Jesus' response to the woman at the well, Nicodemus, Nathaniel, Zaccheus, the Centurion, the woman caught in adultery, Simon the Pharisee, Peter, Andrew, etc. were each different. It was about the same Kingdom no doubt, but Jesus revealed different facets of the Kingdom to each of them that were relevant to their context.

The simple conclusion I came to, is that God is not into legal definitions and neither did He intend His Kingdom and matters of love and faith to be precisely defined. There are boundaries no doubt, like, no matter how much we are a Kingdom and community, and we are to share, I can't come and take your property as mine whenever I like. But it seems abundantly clear to me that God does not want us to focus on rights and obligations or certain criteria to be fulfilled. It is the heart that God is interested in. He's not interested in legalism. For all that the Pharisees did to keep the law, and they did that perfectly from a legal standpoint, they did not know the heart of God, nor did they care about the heart of man.

That comes out clearly in the parable of the prodigal son. Actually, we have given that parable a wrong title. It should be called the parable of the elder son, because the main point of the parable is not the prodigal son, but the sad picture of the elder son. How tragic that the elder son served his father obediently, even slaved for him, but did not know his father's heart. I believe that was the main point Jesus was making to the Jews (Lk.15:11-32).

I was called to the Bar in England and I practiced as a lawyer in Malaysia for 10 years. I argued cases in court and I think I was pretty good at that. I think I knew quite a bit about legal definitions and why it is necessary and how it works, etc. From my understanding of legal text, I can tell you most assuredly that the Bible, the canon of Scripture, a collection of 66 books spanning 1500 years, is not legal text nor was it intended by God to be a legal text spelling out in detail what God authorizes, validates or allows and what He does not. Like, "Where in the Bible does it say that we can drive cars?" We often hear Christians asking, "Where in the Bible does it say that … ?" followed with, "Well, if it is not in the Bible, then it can't be right. That's not from God." They do not seem to realize this, but there is an obvious flaw in that reasoning because if that was the right way of treating the Bible, then we need to first ask, "Where in the Bible does it say that unless something is found in the Bible, then it cannot be treated as true or of God?"

Of course if something we are considering blatantly contravenes or is inconsistent with a command or principle or teaching in Scripture, now that is of course an absolute "No!" But it would be a mistake for theologians and Bible teachers to treat the Bible as a law book and to try to systematize what was never intended to be systematized and define what was never meant to be defined like how we do it in the field of law. *But my point is this – when Christians treat the Bible like a law book then they will live under the law and miss the heart and spirit of the Word and what it means to live by the Spirit.*

Although there is a place for clear lines and boundaries, Jesus on many occasions purposely avoided definitions whenever the Jews asked for one. He was aiming for the heart. He did not want them to become even more legalistic. For example, to the legal expert who wanted to know the extent of his legal obligations, instead of defining who his neighbors were, Jesus turned the question around and focused not on his legal obligations, but on the man in need. Who was neighbor to him? Not a matter of law but a matter of the heart. Neither was Jesus interested in giving us a formula or model because there is none. Jesus is the Gospel!

Over the years I have come to observe that we are more concerned with being right than loving people. Being correct is of utmost importance. Actually living out the truth and loving people is secondary. This all-consuming focus on correct doctrine and being correct was well illustrated by Juan Carlos Ortiz in his book "Disciple". He said to imagine a scenario where people come for a Bible study on joy. They learn everything there is about joy. They examine and compare all the Bible verses on joy. They even debate on what is the correct Biblical definition of joy. Finally after a few hours, they have completed their study and they all go home with their notes and everyone thinks that they know all about joy. But is there really joy in their lives? Nobody seems to be really concerned about that. They are more concerned with whether they have come into a correct and accurate understanding of joy and if they were more correct about joy than someone else.

Making sure we have the correct definition of neighbor and knowing the exact extent of our obligations is everything to most of us. Going and finding out what's happening in other people's lives, especially those in need, and being neighbor to them is … well … secondary. Or maybe it doesn't even cross our minds at all? Jesus said it is by our love that people will know we are His disciples (Jn.13:34-35); not our doctrines or our beliefs. Why is it we are more concerned about being right than living right? Being right is of course important because we do not want to operate on false beliefs, but unless we are actually also living right, we are fooling ourselves if we believe that being right or having the correct knowledge or interpretation of the Bible alone will save us (Jas.1:22). Most Christians are unaware how much we have been influenced by the Greeks, who influenced the Romans, who influenced the whole Western world, who gave us our education. To the Greeks, knowledge is only cognitive, or what we may call "head knowledge". But to the Hebrews, and this is what the Bible tells us – a person does not really know something unless he lives it (1 Jn.2:3-6). All of this boils down to one thing – *just as God can be known (ginosko) only from our hearts, we cannot know His Kingdom except through our hearts.* It is so obvious that I need not mention it, but for the avoidance of doubt, let me make it plain that although the mind is also involved to understand and process what it all means, yet the primary "organ" to know (ginosko) God is not the mind but the heart.

Just one more thing the study and practice of law has helped me understand, is about judgment. Too often we think of God only as a God of mercy and we forget that God is also a God of judgment. Like it or not, there is a judgment for everything and God's judgment is coming to the world. In fact it is already in operation in a way that most people do not realize. While there are people hearing the voice of God speaking in their hearts and waking up to what it means to love God and love our neighbors, others are becoming more and more blind and deaf and hardened, refusing to budge, preserving and defending "Church" as we know it. When people harden their hearts to God, then God will harden their hearts even more and they will become blind and deaf to His voice (Isaiah 6:1-13 and Matt.13:10-15, Mk.4:9-12, Jn.12:35-36, 2 Thess.2:11-12).

Every time the word of God comes to us, whether through a sermon or a book or a conversation, or even just a thought, something happens in our heart. Either we listen and respond in obedience or we make excuses why we will not obey and harden our hearts against what we just heard. Each time the word of God is delivered, it also comes with a judgment. Jesus said, *"You are going to have the light just a little while longer. Walk while you have the light, lest darkness overtake you. The man who walks in the dark does not know where he is going."* (Jn.12:35 NKJV). When we do not make a decision and act upon the word that comes to us, darkness will overtake us. We will become blind. And deaf. And the word of God will no longer have any effect on us (see Jn.12:36-40)

Word, Wonders and Works

Having said the above about definitions, formulas and models, I do however appreciate that we have been brought up with Western secular education. Some people are uneasy with fuzzy ideas and they still need something more concrete, like maybe some clear points describing what the Gospel is, or what the Kingdom is, or what church would look like if it followed what God meant it to be. I certainly do not have the definitive answer for it nor should I be falling foul of what I have so strongly spoken against, but having thought and prayed about it for some years, for simplicity sake, perhaps here are some points I think might describe the Gospel of the Kingdom. This is not a definition or a formula or a model, but I think there would be at least three W's : Word (truth), Wonders (power), and Works (love).

From my observations, most of the evangelical world understand the Gospel only in terms of it being Word (message of good news) – the first **W** : Christians try to tell people that God loves them and they need to be saved.

Then came the Pentecostal and charismatic move of the Holy Spirit. Christians began to realize that the Gospel is not only good news but also signs and wonders. This is the second **W**. Christians wanted not only to tell people, they wanted to demonstrate the reality of God through the power of signs and wonders. The message was not only a God in heaven but also a God actively operating on earth who wants to set you free right now. So the Gospel is not only about future salvation in heaven but present salvation on earth too. Not only do you need to be saved, you need to be set free from demonic power and sicknesses etc. Inner healing also came on the scene – God wants to set you free from mental and emotional bondage too.

It seems to me that much of the church is still on the first **W**. Many have included the second **W** into their theology and understanding of the Gospel, with some practice of it (only some). Many think that's all there is to the Gospel. We think that we have the full Gospel now. We call ourselves "Full Gospel" this and "Full Gospel" that. There is however a third part of the Gospel that the evangelical church at large has yet to realize – and for many years I did not realize it. This is represented by the third **W** : good works. Not just a message of love or the power of God to set you free. *The Gospel is also the love of God in action*. IN FACT THE HEART OF THE GOSPEL IS LOVE.

Because God loves us, He doesn't want us to be separated from Him. Because God loves us, He sent His Son. Because God loves us, He does not want us to continue in bondage and His power to set us free is a demonstration of His love for us. And because God loves us, He is concerned for our well being. God created us to be spirit, soul and body. He is concerned for our whole being. Installing a well for a poor community or starting a health clinic or school in a poor community is not just a good strategy or means to enable us to share the Gospel with the people. The installation of the well and the operating of the health clinic and school by themselves, motivated by God's love, are already part of the Gospel – the Gospel of the Kingdom.

For small group discussion :

1. How do you think people in your nation see the churches in your nation?
2. If for some reason your church were to close down, would it make a difference to the surrounding community? Apart from the members of the church, would anyone in the community miss you?
3. Imagine if someone had asked Jesus what He meant by "church". What do you think He would have replied? In what ways can we be less "churchy" and more community with the people around us?
4. What did Jesus mean by "salt" and "light"? Can God be glorified if you shone out for Him in your work place and made a difference there, and in the lives of the people you work with, although no souls are won into His Kingdom?
5. What are some things you and your friends can do to make a difference in the lives of the poor and needy around you?
6. What was it that crucified Jesus? Why is legalism the anti-thesis to love? Read Lk.15:11-32. How do you think it was possible that the elder son served his father obediently and yet did not know his father's heart like the younger son did?

Chapter 9

Tying Up Some Loose Ends

Then Elisha prayed, "O LORD, please open his eyes so that he may see." Then the LORD opened the servant's eyes, and he looked and saw .. (2Kgs.6:17)

Good Works – Good Strategy?

I think many Christians agree that helping people is good. No one disagrees with that. But not many understand that as part of the Gospel. I believe God wants us to love people practically; not just talk about His love. In fact how can anyone go around talking about God's love but not love? Yes it is a command of the Lord to preach His love, and I am not making any less of that. But do stop for a moment and think about this. Isn't it absurd to just talk about love and not love? Isn't it absurd to tell the poor that God loves them and just leave them in their predicament? (Jas.2:15, 1 Jn.3:16-18). But even more absurd and preposterous I believe is what happens when Christians get into good works as a strategy to preach the Gospel (or to shamelessly promote their church or denomination, or as a feel-good or feel-great self-aggrandizement exercise – which I shall not waste precious space to talk about).

When we see good works only as a strategy for the message of the Gospel, then it will be only that way – just a strategy. People are not stupid. They will know it. They will know we just want to convert them. Can you imagine how you would feel if Muslims did that to us, just to try to win us to become Muslims? Surely we would question how genuine their love is. For everything we do to help people, you can be sure they will question your motive behind it. People know when they are just the "targets" of an evangelistic project or if they are really being loved.

As an example, and something for us to reflect on, here's a true story related to me by the leader of a Christian NGO. After the Tsunami in the Indian Ocean in 2004, their organization gave boats to fishermen who had lost their boats in the Tsunami. A month later, the leader went to visit the area to check if the boats were still there or if the fishermen had sold it off or something. As he stood on the beach taking photos of the boats floating on the water, he realized a fisherman was standing next to him observing him. As he turned to the fisherman, the fisherman said to him, "I know why you gave us boats but you did not give us nets." He was somewhat surprised, so he asked the fisherman, "Why?" The fisherman answered, "Because you can put the name of your organization on a boat, but you cannot put it on a net."

But the main thing is not so much how people will interpret us, but this – are we or are we not genuinely loving people without any ulterior motive? Jesus told us to be salt and light simply because of who we are – children of our Father in heaven. He did not tell us to be salt and light in order that it would create a platform or bridge for us to win souls to Him. Yes, often (though not always) being salt and light will open the door into people's hearts that will give us the opportunity to share the message of the Gospel with them. If that happens, great, but that is not the Biblical motive for being salt and light, is it? I have to confess that there was a time when I did approach it that way. But as my understanding of the Kingdom of God grew, I asked myself if Jesus would have done that. I went back to study the sermon on the mount and discovered how wrong I had been.

In the community development/transformation training I have been conducting, this is the emphasis – if we really understand that love is not a strategy, and good works is in itself a part of the Gospel, as much as the message of John 3:16 is a part of the Gospel, and as much as God's power to set free is a part of the Gospel, then I believe the Kingdom of God will come into a community. All three are necessary. Otherwise we are not bringing the full Gospel to people.

How much do most churches around the world understand this? The statistics of how much churches give to the poor (Appendix 1) speak for themselves. Even churches that are very mission minded talk of church planting only in terms of the first and second W. Church planting is centered in meetings. Any kind of community projects is seen only as incidental and as a strategy. When I talk of community projects, immediately most churches will think that it costs too much money and too much time and effort, and the time would better be spent doing "outreach, preaching and teaching". They do not see that good clean and safe drinking water, children learning Math and English, and the creation of work opportunities so that parents can work to earn good profits, so that they can feed their children well and not be enslaved to money lenders – that all these are also a very essential part of church, meaning community (see the Ghana story in Appendix 6). The amazing thing is, we believe all this is absolutely necessary for ourselves and our own children, but not for the people we are trying to reach. Why?

In extending the blessings of Abraham, and in being concerned for what God is concerned, we must be concerned for the whole person. That ultimately involves restoration of their image as children of God, and recovery of their vocation as productive stewards of God's creation. It also involves restoration of their ability to stand on their own feet and have the dignity of true children of God. In

arrived
10/29/15

our efforts to "win over the lost" we must not take nutrition, shelter, water, education, health care, etc as just a means of reaching people with the Gospel. All these – nutrition, shelter, water, education, health care, a means of livelihood, etc. are part of the Gospel and ought to be part of our mission. God cares and He has sent us to care irrespective of whether people respond to our message. Of course we desire that people be reconciled to God and that their eternal future be secured, but love must be unconditional. Should we not do our part in loving unconditionally and leave the results to God?

If we understand the reason why God created us and we understand the Kingdom, and we understand that the Gospel of the Kingdom is not just a message, then instead of employing any strategies (including business strategies) or means, as a bridge or platform for the Gospel, and instead of trying to "plant a church", we would go and simply *share our lives* with people who do not know Jesus. This will obviously include both the spiritual as well as helping them with livelihood, health, education, agriculture, technical knowledge, government, etc.

If our desire is to see people set free and reconciled to God and for them to discover who they really are – the sons and daughters of the Most High God, gifted to be and do much more than they can think or imagine, and if we desire to see them reach their full potential and become a strength and blessing to others in their community, and if we desire to see the Kingdom of God come into individuals, families, communities and nations, then discipling nations would be *a sharing of lives, and lives influencing lives* (in all aspects – spiritual, physical, mental, emotional – personal, family, community, social, cultural, corporate, national, international and global). Not just evangelism, Bible study, church planting or discipleship of individuals.

Not of this world?

In Jn.17:14 and 16, Jesus said that His disciples are not of this world just as He is not of this world. Further in Jn.18:36, Jesus said His Kingdom is not of this world. What did He mean by that? Does this negate all that we have been looking at in terms of God's Kingdom on earth? Certainly not.

The first thing we must bear in mind is that Jesus clearly told His disciples that He is not taking them out of the world but sending them into the world (Jn.17:15,18). Second, note that Jesus was responding to Pilate who was questioning Jesus' authority (Jn.18:33,35. See also Jn.19:10-11). In contrast to Pilate's authority which came from man, what Jesus was saying is that His authority did not come from man, nor from this world, but from "another place" ("realm" NASB).

Imagine what Jesus was facing at that point. This was the end of His mission on earth. He was going to leave His disciples and pass the baton to them to continue on His mission after His death. He also knew that the enemy was going to stir up the political and religious powers of this world to come against Him, and against His disciples after He is killed. How would He face the inevitable? Would He defend Himself? Would He call on the powers of heaven to destroy them? Or would He love till His last breath, forgive those who came against Him, and willingly lay down His life? What would happen to His disciples in this crisis? How would they face the enemy and the powers in this world and carry on without Him? How would the Kingdom of God come through them? It is in this context that we must understand Jesus' prayer in John 17 and the events of John 18.

There is no doubt that God wants His Kingdom to be established on earth (Matt.6:10). Jesus announced that at the start of His ministry. And in Matt.11:12, Jesus said the Kingdom of heaven was forcefully advancing on earth. One day, God will get what He set out to do from the time He first put man on earth. The kingdom of this world will become the Kingdom of Jesus Christ (Rev.11:15). But God's way for this to happen is not through human striving and fighting for power and dominion, nor through political campaigning, maneuvering, and manipulation. Instead, the way of the Kingdom of God is opposite to the ways of this world (Lk.22:25-26). In other words, Jesus was telling Pilate that He was not going to play politics with him. And neither were His disciples to do so.

In direct opposition to the value systems of this world, Jesus said the greatest in the Kingdom is the servant. God's Kingdom will advance through love overcoming hatred, good overcoming evil, humility overcoming pride, giving rather than taking, blessing when we are cursed, offering the other cheek when we are struck, winning through losing, and living through dying. See Rev.12:10-11. It is in this way that the disciples of Christ, like their Master, are not of this world, meaning not of the spirit, culture and values of this world. That is why Jesus said, *"My kingdom is not of this world. If it were, my servants would fight to prevent my arrest by the Jews .."* (Jn.18:36).

In the same way when Paul, James, Peter and John spoke of "the wisdom of the world", "the spirit of the world", "the weapons of the world", "the basic principles of the world", "a friend of the world", "the corruption of the world", and "viewpoint of the world", they were speaking of the culture and values of this world. It is not the world we are to avoid, or withdraw or separate ourselves from, but the ways of the world that we are not to follow. How else can we possibly be salt and light if we do not penetrate into the world? Jesus said that no one lights a lamp and puts it under a cover (Matt.5:15). Clearly, He did not intend for us to withdraw from this world. This has already been addressed at length in Chapter 7. Instead, we are left as lights in this world to continue Jesus' mission (Jn.17:18, 20:21), to permeate the world with the truth, culture and values of God's Kingdom like how yeast would work through the whole dough (Lk.13:20-21). Thus we are to be in the world but not of it.

The sad irony however is that the church today is not in the world (because we have largely withdrawn from having a voice and any relevance or impact in the world) but we are of it, because though we have withdrawn from the world, the world is still so much in us. How else can we explain the fact of more than 41,000 denominations to this world? Not to mention the politics of money and power within many churches, nor the worldly ways by which many churches and TV evangelists try to get people into church or to donate money?

What About the Message?

No doubt you might be wondering with all this emphasis on love and being salt and light and transforming cultures, what about the truth? Or what about the message of the Gospel? Please understand that I am in no way making any less of the need for truth and neither am I neglecting the command to proclaim the message of the Gospel. I am going to say something I believe is vital about proclamation, but first consider this. Not everyone responded to Jesus, but think of the people in the Gospels who did : Peter, John, Andrew, the woman caught in adultery, the woman at the well, etc. Was it because they came into a cognitive understanding of the truth or was it because they came to *experience Jesus Who is the Truth*? I will return to this point later, but do stop and reflect on this for a moment.

There is so much deception in this world. And obviously some people are more deceived than others. But whether more or less, all men have been blinded by Satan the god of this world (2 Cor.4:4). People need the truth. Only the truth will set people free (Jn.8:32). The general command to us is to proclaim the message of the Gospel. We should be ever ready to do that. But what is the message of the Gospel? Though conveniently reduced down to "Four things God wants you to know", the message of the Gospel is however much more than that. From Lk.9:2 and 6 we see that the message of the Gospel is "the Kingdom of God". That means that it encompasses all that God wants us to know about life in His Kingdom as He intended it to be, made possible by Jesus Christ. It is something we will continue to learn even after we have accepted Jesus as our Savior.

In Jn.17:3 Jesus did not describe eternal life as being in heaven, nor in terms of time, but in terms of relationship. Eternal life is knowing God the Father and knowing Jesus the Son. To know God is to know His heart and all He desires for us. As I mentioned in Chapter 6, the Gospel of the Kingdom traces back to Genesis and spells out what God created us for in the first place and what it means to be in His Kingdom. In other words the message we are to share is not about Jesus saving us from hell to give us a place in heaven after we die. No doubt the truth about salvation from eternal damnation is an essential part of the message, but the Gospel is not just about escaping hell or about leaving this world for another better world. The Gospel is a call to repent and be part of God's Kingdom – and it starts with being in His Kingdom on earth. What good news of the Kingdom have you been telling people?

Since the message of the Gospel is so extensive, how much are we to share each time? Are there core truths that must be shared each time? Is there an irreducible minimum? I don't believe there is, nor would that be the right approach.

God knows exactly what's going on in the heart and mind of each person and He alone knows what each person needs to hear and when they need to hear it, or if at all. Not only does action speak louder than words, sometimes silence may speak louder than words. And so, like Jesus, I believe we need to seek the heart of our Father and speak only what the Father tells us. And we need to trust the Holy Spirit to work in the hearts of people in the way only He knows what and how (Jn.3:8, Mk.1:35. Mk.6:46, Lk.5:16, Lk.6:12, Jn.5:17-20,30, Jn.8:28-29, Jn.12:49-50, Jn.20:21).

It goes without saying that even when truth needs to be spoken, truth is not a package with each package having the same contents. Not only must we remember that God may use different people to break up the hard ground, to water and soften the soil, to plant the seed, to water the seed, etc., each person who encountered Jesus encountered a different facet of the Truth. They had different things to be set free from. Going even further, not only was Jesus in no hurry to preach the whole truth to anyone, the basic thing was that He is the Truth and He simply lived out who He is.

If the Truth is a Person, not just a historical figure, and He is actively seeking out those who will return to Him, and His Spirit lives in us, and we are to be the primary conduit by which people will come to know Him, then the fundamental question that must be asked is, "Do people see Jesus in us?" Peter said to live godly lives and be ready to give to everyone an answer for the reason for our hope (1 Pet.3:15). Why would anyone ask us the reason for our hope unless we are obviously living lives that go against the current of this world? But more than that, we are called to know Jesus and have more of Him in us (Jn.3:30, Gal.2:20) and have His life fragrance spread around us (2 Cor.2:14-16). So it is not just a question of living out what we believe and preaching by our lives and hoping for an opportunity to tell them the message of the Gospel or hoping people will ask us. It is more a question of simply walking with Jesus, and then who He is – the Way, the Truth and the Life – will naturally be seen and felt by people who encounter us.

I have come to realize that it is not about preaching this or that or anything, nor about using techniques to convince people, nor about preaching at all; but we would be preaching and coming against the deception, spirit and values of this world without even being conscious of it if we would walk with Him. That's the basic thing. John said we are to walk as He walked. In this world we are to be like Him (1 Jn.4:17), walking with the Father and showing Jesus and the Father by our lives. And from time to time, we will speak as we are led by His Spirit, which could be a gentle word or a direct challenge or even a strong rebuke.

Even when we share, it is not so much an objective truth or a historical Jesus that we are to share. Rather, it is Jesus the Truth that we personally know that we are to share. I believe that is what it means to be His witnesses. If people do not get so much as a whiff of Jesus from us, then we really have nothing to speak of. I wonder how much, if at all, people see or smell Jesus in me? Am I just a good talker to most people?

I am not saying we need to attain some "level" of holiness before we can share the message of the Gospel. Often the best people who bring others to Christ are new believers themselves. They are simply spreading their new-found joy. Michael Green said that we ought to regard sharing the message of the Gospel like one beggar telling another beggar where to find bread. That I must say is such an apt metaphor that should also guard us against an "I know, you don't" or "I'm right, you're wrong" approach to sharing the message. But I hope you get the point I am making here – we are to share the *now* Jesus, the Jesus we personally know; not just the historical Jesus, an objective truth among so many other beliefs that this world can choose from. We have to be witnesses of what we say, meaning not just delivering a message but sharing what we personally know to be true.

Of course none of us live a perfect life and we surely don't have to wait until we feel we do before we share the message of the Gospel, but unless we are the living Bible to people, why would they be interested in reading what we proclaim? We need to ask ourselves if *we* are good news in the first place. As my friend and mentor Joe Ozawa often asks, "How can we bring the good news if we are the bad news to them?" It is well known that Gandhi (who was inspired by his reading of Jesus' life and death, upon which he based his struggle for independence with non-violent acts of civil disobedience) said, "If it were not for the Christians in India, India would be Christian." Another Indian, a Bengali Brahmin once said, "If only the Christians in India were more interested in me than in my soul, India would be Christian."

God can use a donkey to speak for Him if He wants to (Num.22:28), but that is not His primary objective. Because the Truth is a person – Jesus Christ, not a concept or philosophy or belief, and because the Truth is about life and love, God desires that we, who have been made in His image, would like His Son, "flesh out" the truth of life and love to others. Then there would be, not dissonance, but harmony between the words we speak and the life we live. And living truth will reproduce living truth.

I still retain the hope that in my loving people, I would have the opportunity to share with them the message. But I am not looking or waiting for an angle. Instead I believe I need to be more focused on loving and praying for God to reveal Himself to the people He sends me to love. With more and more advertisement claims being made each day through the ever expanding reach of the media, and with more and more reports of the moral failure of leaders in government, in religious and other traditionally trusted institutions, it seems that the whole world is infected with cynicism and skepticism. Most people are asking – is there anything really authentic in the world today? Where are the people who truly walk the talk? Indeed the whole of creation is waiting in eager expectation for the true children of God to be revealed (Rom.8:19)

Three other things need to be addressed : 1) What about the apostle Paul? 2) How should we as the church go and love the poor? 3) What about suffering?

Often, theologians who have been challenged to consider the ramifications of the Kingdom Gospel, have a question : Why was Paul so focused on his central theme of salvation by grace that it appears that he had little or almost no regard for a Kingdom Gospel or ministry? Could it be that the greatest apostle of all "missed" it, or that those of us who are now advocating for this paradigm shift are terribly mistaken? I have addressed this point in Appendix 7.

As to how we should love as the church, I beg you not to make the mistake of trying to love as an institution. I have addressed this point in Appendix 8.

If God loves us and wants His Kingdom on earth, why does He allow suffering? It doesn't make sense that God would send us to be agents of transformation so that things can be put right but at the same time He is letting things get out of hand. And why do bad things happen to even those who love and serve Him? Why did God even put the tree of knowledge of good and evil in the Garden of Eden in the first place? Didn't He know what would result from that? I have addressed these questions in Appendix 10.

For small group discussion :

1. Jesus talked about giving in secret (Matt.6:3-4). Some kids in India learnt this in Sunday school. They decided to fast every morning, and pool their money together to help the poor. They bought blankets for street kids who slept in the cold on the floors of the train station. In the morning the street kids would wake up not knowing who had covered them with a blanket the previous night. Someone who heard about this said, "Oh what a waste! That's no use if the Christian kids did not make themselves known and make it known that they are Christians." What do you think?

2. There are many who still hold strongly to the belief that Christians should have nothing to do with this world. How would they reconcile that with Jesus sending us into the world and the call to be salt and light and with God's desire for His Kingdom to come and His will to be done on earth as in heaven, and for His Kingdom to advance on earth?

3. Someone said this when he was talking about evangelism, "The problem with Christians all over the world is that they are always trying to answer questions that people are not asking." What do you think?

4. If only God knows what is in each person's heart and mind, and if only the Holy Spirit can bring revelation and conviction, and bring about a spiritual re-birth (Jn.3:8), how can we be more sensitive to Jesus' voice (Matt.10:27) and to the leading of the Holy Spirit (Rom.8:14)?

5. The next time you share the Gospel with someone, how would you share the Gospel of the Kingdom with him/her?

Chapter 10

It's About God's Heart

It's not really about the poor or about transformation. It's about God's heart and His Kingdom. The heart and end goal of the Gospel are people crazily in love with Jesus.

She Gave All

If you have read up to this point and you are still having a hard time trying get a handle on what the Kingdom is, then I want to encourage you to cease trying to understand it only cognitively but to open your heart to the Lord, for it is only by our hearts (ginosko – a love union with the Lord) that we can come to know God and experience His Kingdom. Without that, we can try to be as precise and as accurate as we can in coming out with a definition, but for all the accuracy, we can miss the heart of the matter. So I want to come to the heart of the matter. This is not another W. Or maybe it is : Wife! ☺ This, I would say, is what the Gospel is ultimately all about – it is about falling crazily in love with Jesus and giving all of our heart and life to Him. Jesus did not come just to save souls from hell. He came to get a bride for Himself.

There is a passage recorded in all the Gospels that is very intriguing. It tells of an incident in which an unknown woman came up to Jesus and poured out her affection on Jesus in a very dramatic way. In response, Jesus told all the people who witnessed this incident, *"Truly I tell you, wherever the gospel is preached throughout the world, what she has done will also be told, in memory of her."* (Matt.26:13) See corresponding passages in Mark14:3-9, Matt.26:6-13, Lk.7:36-47, Jn.11:1-2, Jn.12:1-7, Lk.10:38-42

Who was this woman? Why did she show such an outpouring of affection on Jesus? And why did Jesus say that wherever the Gospel is preached, what she did will also be told in memory of her? Have any of us done that? Many of us have preached the Gospel many times, but have any of us in sharing the Gospel ever added to it this story of what she did? What is the connection between the Gospel and what she did? Could it be that we have been missing something vital? Could it be that our understanding of the Gospel falls short of what Jesus meant by the Gospel?

To find answers to this, first we need to ask if there is anything in the Gospels that might give us a clue as to why this woman would show such an outpouring of affection on Jesus. Perhaps there is. I believe it is very possible that this woman could very well be the same woman who was caught in adultery in the account in Jn 8:1-11. There is a hint in the Luke passage that lends some weight to this. Luke describes her as a woman who had a lived a very sinful life. And Simon the leper thinks to himself, *"If this man were a prophet, he would know who is touching him and what kind of woman she is – that she is a sinner."*

Here's the scenario. Her partner got away with not even a mention. She however was caught and dragged out to be humiliated and killed in public. Where were all her "lovers"? Did no one love her enough to come forward to speak up on her behalf? This was the crunch. Not only was she shamefully exposed, she was being condemned to death. In her hour of crisis, condemned to the punishment of being stoned to death, no one showed her the kind of love like Jesus did. Not only did Jesus save her from being stoned to death, we can imagine how touched she was by Jesus' kindness and love. That could give the background to why one day, she could hold it no longer. She just suddenly showed up uninvited, unannounced, and lavished her love upon Jesus. Her breaking of the alabaster box and the outpouring of the perfume symbolized so dramatically the breaking and outpouring of her passion from deep within her for Jesus.

It is quite possible too that this woman was Mary Magdalene who apparently had a close relationship with the Lord. That however is another issue, which unfortunately has been twisted in the Da Vincci Code (sadly although Dan Brown himself says that it is work of fiction many people have taken what he says as fact). OK, irrespective of whether that was Mary Magdalene or someone else, we can understand that Jesus would have been touched by her dramatic show of gratitude. But Jesus makes no mention of that. Instead He links what she did with the Gospel. *What is the connection between her show of affection and the Gospel?*

I could be wrong, but this is how I read it. I believe this is the picture that Jesus was giving us of the end goal of the Gospel – of a woman pouring out her love and passion upon Jesus. This is what the Gospel is all about. It is not so much about eternal salvation as it is about God's long lost bride forsaking all other loves, leaving her adultery, and returning to Him and lavishing her love upon her Bridegroom. Throughout the ages, God has been looking for a bride – a people who will fall hopelessly in love with Him – a people who will forsake all, give all and lose themselves in response to His love.

John Eldredge in 'Wild At Heart' and with his wife Stasi in 'Captivating : Unveiling the Mystery of a Woman's Soul' says, *"In the heart of every man is a desperate desire for a battle to fight, an adventure to live, and a beauty to rescue .. Every woman longs for three things : to be swept up into a romance, to play an irreplaceable role in a great adventure, and to be the Beauty of the story."* Think of almost any exciting feel good movie you've watched. Why is it that it almost always has the same recurrent theme – there's always a near-death crisis, a battle or struggle involved, with a villain, a beautiful maiden in distress, and a good guy hero who overcomes incredible odds at the peril of his own life to rescue her, and in the end he gets his woman and they ride off into the sunset? Though the stories vary, the theme remains almost the same, but we never tire of it, do we? Could it not be that it is in fact the very love story of God's great love for us that He has embedded in every human heart? (Eccl.3:11).

Unfortunately most of what church is today has been built around nothing more than "fire insurance". Sadly, evangelical Christianity's focus on salvation seems to appreciate nothing else for why Jesus came, except to save us from hell. Evangelical Christianity that makes correct doctrine its cornerstone has no idea of a Jesus who came to die and win back His bride for Himself. The Gospel is not just about salvation from something. It is also about salvation to something or Someone. There's more to abundant life than all that I talked about previously.

Why did God create us in the first place? Why a man and a woman – a husband and wife, as the image of God? Why did God call Israel His wife? Why did God say that Israel had committed adultery against Him? Were these just strange inappropriate metaphors that crazy wild eyed prophets conjured up in their minds on their own, or could it be that they understood just how hurt and jealous God felt for us and how passionately He longs for us to return to Him?

How does God Love Us?

What do we know of God's love? Suppose I were to say to you, "God loves you." What would come to your mind? God's provision of food and shelter for you? His giving you a good family? His protection over you daily? His dying on the cross for you, saving you from hell, and giving you eternal life? These are what most Christians would think about when they think about God's love for them. In the Bible however, God's love for us is described not only in terms of how He cares for us and provides for us, and how He saves us and gives us eternal life, but also in romantic terms :

> *As a bridegroom rejoices over his bride, so will your God rejoice over you.* (Isa.62:5)

> *I have loved you with an everlasting love. Therefore with lovingkindness I have drawn you to Myself.* (Jer.31:3)

> *The Lord your God will take great delight in you. He will quiet you with His love. He will rejoice over you with singing.* (Zeph.3:17)

Various pictures are given to us in the Bible of God's relationship with us : Shepherd and sheep, Master and servant, Commander of the Army and soldiers, Vine and branches, Potter and clay, etc. but the final picture in the Book of Revelation is the Bridegroom and His Bride. That is really the ultimate relationship the Lord seeks from us. Right from the very beginning we were made in the image of God – male and female (not only male) (Gen.5:2). In our earthly human relationship with each other as males and females, we have a picture and understanding of the relationship that God seeks from us. All through the Old Testament, God spoke of Israel as his wife who had deserted Him and committed adultery with other lovers.

God desires a passionate relationship with us. God longs to be intimate with us and us with Him. Eternal life is described by Jesus not in terms of length of time, but as "knowing" (Greek : *ginosko*) God (Jn.17:3). That is the same Greek word used for how Adam knew Eve his wife, in the Septuagint (the Greek Old Testament). In other words, eternal life is an intimate relationship with God. And this ties back to what was said earlier about knowing God's heart. If we know God, if we love Him, we would feel His heart and His love for people, and there would be a natural love in our hearts for others. The heart of the Gospel is love.

What do Christians today understand of being filled with the Spirit? Being filled with the Holy Spirit is usually understood only in terms of power and anointing; not intimacy with God or love for others. I wonder how many Christians have experienced being filled with God's love.

Have you ever fallen in love before? When you fall in love, madly in love, you become crazy. You become beside yourself. All decorum is swept aside for a display of what is raging in your heart. I believe that this is the crazy love that God is looking for. Does the present-day church understand this?

First Love

We might think it strange, but it is quite possible that someone can be committed and zealous for God but not know Him personally. Paul said of the Jews, *"For I can testify about them that they are zealous for God, but their zeal is not based on knowledge."* (Rom.10:2). Paul himself knew this – when Jesus appeared to Paul the first time, he asked, *"Who are You Lord?"* (Acts 9:5). Here's the elder son again (Lk.15:11-32).

Though the Ephesian church was zealous for Jesus and totally committed to Him, yet they had *"left their first love"* (Rev.2:1-7). Look at how Jesus described the church of Ephesus. Is there any church you know of today that comes close to the dedication, commitment and zeal of the Ephesian church as described by Jesus Himself? I was baffled, so one day I asked the Lord what He meant by "first love". In reply, the Lord asked me, "How did you love your wife when you first fell in love with her?" Ha! I immediately understood. I remembered how I longed to be with her all the time, how I could not bear being apart from her, how I would be dying to see her again whenever we had to be separated even for a few hours, how hours with her would feel like just minutes, how I delighted in her, how I dreamt of her all the time with open eyes, how crazy I was about her .... Yes, there was a time when I loved Jesus this way. Do I still love Jesus this way?

Mary not Martha

Jesus is not looking for Marthas, but for Marys (Lk.10:38-42). God does not just want commitment and a sense of duty from us. In Jn.4:24, John says that God seeks worshippers. In Acts13:22, it says that God found David a man after His own heart. What was it about David that God could say that of him? David said, *"One thing I ask of the LORD, this is what I seek : that I may dwell in the house of the LORD all the days of my life, to gaze upon the beauty of the LORD and to seek 6him in his temple."* (Ps.27:4). Not 5 things, not 3 things, but 1 thing. In Ps.63:1 David said, *"O God, you are my God, earnestly I seek you; my soul thirsts for you, my body longs for you, in a dry and weary land where there is no water."*

I believe that God wants us to go to Him in prayer not just to request and petition Him for things, but to enjoy being with Him, expressing our love for Him. That is what God ultimately desires of us – knowing His love and loving Him in return, as a bride would be in love with her bridegroom. Just enraptured in love and delighting in each other. God will not be satisfied with anything less than all of our hearts : *Search for me with all your heart* (Jer.29:13). *Return to Me with all your heart* (Joel 2:12). *Trust in the Lord with all your heart* (Pr.3:5-6). *Love the Lord with all your heart* (Mark 12:30).

Jesus reminded the Pharisees that life is not found in the knowledge of the Scriptures. Life is found in Jesus. Jesus told the Pharisees : *"You diligently study the Scriptures because you think that by them you possess eternal life. These are the Scriptures that testify about me, yet you refuse to come to me to have life."* (Jn.5:39-40). Someone said this : "The Word did not become a philosophy, theory or a concept to be discussed, debated or pondered. The Word became a person to be followed, enjoyed and loved."

We were designed to have ongoing communion with God, drawing life and love from Him and to hear Him speak to us. Paul says it is those who are led by the Spirit who are the sons of God (Rom.8:14). I often wondered how the Pharisees came to be what they were. I also wondered what happened in the history of the church that caused the church to lose the vibrancy, life and dynamism that it originally had. And how despite wonderful revivals that have occurred in the history of the church, none of them have lasted. Each time, the revival and euphoria not only died away, but the church slumped back into mediocrity and sadly went back to business as usual. Why is that?

I believe it has to do with how we live. There are three ways to live : by the Spirit (spirit and truth), or by principles alone, or by rules and regulations. When there is no ongoing communion with Him, we will descend into living by principles only. That is not a bad thing, but that is not the fullness of what He intended for us. If we are not in constant communion with Him, gradually, even that is lost and we descend into living by law.

Every now and then, God raises up someone to bring people back to Him. However, few people learn from them how to commune with God and hear Him speaking and being led by the Spirit. So the only legacy they leave behind are their teachings which turn into spiritual principles that their followers hang on to. Eventually even these principles are lost and the church makes rules and regulations and follow systems. There is a spiritual lesson for us to heed in how Moses told the Israelites to go and collect fresh manna every morning. Those who thought they could save on work and collected extra to keep for the next day, found their collection had turned rotten. We must have Him and His love afresh every day.

Like newlyweds, when this love rages on in our hearts, it will compel us to be fools for Christ. Paul spoke of even being mad : *"If we are out of our mind, it is for God; if we are in our right mind, it is for you. For Christ's love compels us .."* (2Cor.5:13-14). True ministry is an outflow of this love.

How can we have this love? Dare we ask God for it? When a woman marries a man, she surrenders herself completely to him. She henceforth no longer belongs to any other, not even herself but to him. No doubt the liberated women of today would be upset with this, but I believe that that is because there is so little real love these days. I dare say things would immediately change if someone who would die for his woman were to show up in her life. That of course is our Jesus. The question for us is this : Are we willing to be possessed by His love with all the consequences that follow – that we will lose ourselves and our lives to Him?

Who Was This Woman?

So much of teaching in church encourages people to love more, to pray more, to fast more, to evangelize more, study more of the Bible, give more, attend more of this, get involved in more of that, go on more mission trips, etc. but where do we find the impetus to do more of all these? I see many church workers especially flat out trying to keep up with more of everything. It is no wonder that for many people, if we were to ask them what their picture of God is, quite honestly they will tell you it is Someone sitting supreme on His throne demanding more holiness and more of everything from us.

How about a change of picture? I want to share with you the Jesus who loves you romantically, who even now longs for you to just be alone with Him and immerse yourself in His love. And when you catch His love you are just bursting in your heart to go out and love people, especially the poor. It all begins with Jesus. Drawing near to Him, knowing His heart, sharing His heart, compelled by his love. Not some criteria to be fulfilled so that we are saved. Not some obligation to be fulfilled to be truly Christian. Do we know Him? Do we love Him?

Who was this woman? This woman is the true church, His bride, who loves Him like crazy, that Jesus is coming back for. And the Gospel of the Kingdom is about this King and His bride who loves Him absolutely, and they carry in their hearts His love for one another – God's "love triangle" – and they live happily ever after!

For small group discussion :

1. Having read the previous chapters on love and community, and being the agents of God's Kingdom advance and transformation in this world, how does this chapter relate to the previous chapters?
2. What is your experience of God's love?
3. Why does the author challenge his readers with the dare to ask God for this crazy, passionate love?
4. In Appendix 5, the author said this : *"salvation by grace includes God fulfilling His own law by living in us and through us"*. How does this relate to God's love and being in His Kingdom?
5. What is the end goal of the Gospel? How much do you want it?

Epilogue

There are other insights I would like to share about the Kingdom but to keep this book short and concise I have focused only on God's love as the heart and soul of His Kingdom. In Matt.25 in the parable of the ten virgins (Does anyone doubt Jesus was talking about the church?), Jesus said that all ten virgins fell asleep. All ten of them! We must examine our hearts. Does His love rage in our hearts or have our hearts become cold? I could be wrong, but if I am hearing God right, I believe that we are close to midnight and the call is already going out throughout the earth for us to wake up to the Bridegroom and to His coming Kingdom.

Phil Butler said there are four kinds of hearers : believers, seekers, the indifferent and the antagonistic. "Believers" are those who jump right in. "Seekers" are those who are cautious. They are not easily convinced, but they want to know more before they decide. The "indifferent" don't care. You can do everything you can to try and convince them but you can't get a response from them. Jesus called them "lukewarm". The "antagonistic" oppose you. Often they oppose without truly understanding what you are saying. As you probably can tell, this book is only for believers and seekers*. If you are a believer or seeker and the message in this book has rocked or overturned your boat, you might be asking, "What's next?", "What should I do?" or "What can I do?" Here are some suggestions I would like to make from my own journey :

1. Time
Start with setting aside time to be alone with God and seek to know His heart. Everything begins from that. All the ills of the world began with man being alienated from God. Let's return to Him. I mean really immerse and soak yourself in His presence. And delight yourself in Him. Ask Him to share

His heart with you and fill you with His love. If you have never experienced it before, open your heart to the Bridegroom and fall in love with Him. If you already know what that is, fall in love with Him all over again! Unless we are compelled by His love, all is human striving. Being has to precede doing. It is your heart He wants. Not what you can do for Him.

2. Trust

There is an inherent fear in seeking God. It is fear of the unknown. People want to be close to God but not too close. We are naturally afraid of what "demands" God may make on us. But step back for a moment and ask yourself, "Who else can we trust if not God?" If we cannot trust our Maker, we might as well not be alive. God is love. And despite everything that is wrong, God retains control over all. Bring your fears and insecurities to the Lord. And trust Him totally. Perfect love casts out all fear (1 Jn.4:18).

3. Alignment

As you commune with God and begin to feel His heart, you will be brought into a re-evaluation of who you are and what you really believe. Re-evaluate what it is that you really believe (not what you think you believe), and what's really important and valuable to you. Are they the same as how God would value them? What are you living for? How important are people to you? How important are the poor to you? What about your business or your career? Are they totally under the Lordship of Christ? The pearl merchant and the one who found buried treasure went through a radical re-evaluation of what really mattered to them (Matt.13:44-45).

Reflect and re-evaluate. Begin to align yourself to what He shares with you from His heart. No doubt radical adjustments will have to be made. Time, talent, work, career, relationships, possessions, attachments, ambitions, dreams … Jonah learnt that those who cling to worthless idols forfeit the grace that could be theirs (Jon.2:8). Jim Eliot said, "He is no fool who gives what he cannot keep to gain what he cannot lose." God has to be made Lord of all. Everything has to be subsumed into His Kingdom. Not grudgingly, but joyfully, compelled by His love.

4. Look Out

Expand your horizons. The world is a much bigger place than your immediate world. Get a vision from God of His Kingdom and see how your talents can make a difference to the lives of other people, especially the needy. We were meant to be community. Team up with others who share the same heart.

You may be in a position to influence and effect change at the corporate or even national level that will have a positive impact on society especially for the marginalized. Or you may be in a position to influence just a few individuals around you. But at whatever level you might be functioning for God's Kingdom advance, I encourage you to ask God to show you the needy and to lead you to engage with them on a personal basis. It doesn't have to be someone on the other side of the planet. It could be right around the corner from where you live or work. Or team up with those who are already working among the poor in the hard places of this world. Don't just give money. Get involved personally. If Jesus the King of kings could come down from His throne to be with the poor … well, I guess I don't have to complete this sentence.

5. Step out

Every belief calls for action. Cowards have no place in His Kingdom (Rev.21:7). God called Abraham out. Jesus called Peter out. Everyone who was instrumental in God's plans and purposes was called to step out of their security. Abraham had to leave Haran. Peter had to step out of his boat. Your boat is all that keeps you afloat. It is all that you are familiar with. Until action follows belief, James says mere belief is deceptive. God calls people to step out so that He alone is their anchor, their source, and their captain. No plan B but Him. Get engaged with the needs of others – with those whom the Lord leads you to. Those He puts on your heart.

A word of caution here – giving money alone to the poor will not really help them. It may in fact create dependency and reinforce their poverty. The poor need your friendship more than your money. Email me if you are already working among the poor and you want to know how to help them out of poverty.

6. Walk

Keep your eyes on the Lord. One step at a time. Constantly checking your compass and re-aligning. Using another metaphor (from my friend Alex Araujo) be a sailboat, not a power-boat, and let the wind of the Spirit take you to where He will. It will be a journey of discovery. Knowing more and more of His heart. Learning more and more of His love. Feeling His love for others. Discovering more of yourself. Learning what it means to be in God's community. Learning to die to self as you put others first. Learning the joy of giving and being instrumental for His Kingdom.

7. Rest

When you go against the current of this world, you can be sure you will meet up with opposition. Remain anchored to Jesus and stand strong against the current, but also rest in Him. That which is born of the flesh is flesh. That which is born of the Spirit is Spirit (Jn.3:6). Human striving cannot accomplish God's plans and advance His Kingdom. Only the

Spirit can. He will establish His plans for you and through you in His own time.

If you are a leader of a church or Christian group, and you are also asking the question, "What's next?" here are some questions you might want to consider as a church/group in addition to the points above (which also apply to a church or group) :

1. How much are we a community? How much are we engaged in God's Kingdom advance?

2. What are the things that encourage community and Kingdom advance, and what are the things that do not or that actually hinder community and Kingdom advance?

3. Wolfgang Simson says, "Church as we know it, is preventing church as God wants it." How prepared are we to make radical adjustments to throw out the things that are not helpful or hinder community and Kingdom advance, and to come into alignment with God's intentions?

Jesus had only 12 disciples. He discipled them to disciple others (Jn.13:34-35, 21:15-17). Paul who told us to follow him as he followed Jesus did likewise with small teams everywhere he went, making not only disciples but disciplers – those who will disciple others (2Tim.2:2). God has designed us to be seeds and cells that multiply. We are not called the Body of Christ for no reason. Seeds and cells that do not multiply are dead (Jn.12:24-26). Discipleship is not a class or program or church service, but lives influencing lives.

If Jesus discipled only 12, how many do you think you can disciple at one time? Why did Jesus disciple only 12? Why not 50 or 200 or 2000? Most people think it probably has to do with the 12 tribes of Israel. Perhaps. But I think the true reason is simply because love and influence requires time and attention. Why 12 is like asking the question, "How many children can you have?" In Asia, those with more than 10 children often can't remember the birthdays of their children. Some can't even remember the names of their children! When Jesus said *"I am the way .."* (Jn.14:6) I believe He was talking not only about salvation. Jesus has set the pattern for us for how we are to walk with the Father and how we are to do ministry. He said, *"As the Father has sent Me, I send you."* (Jn.20:21). Why follow Constantine? Why not follow Jesus? How prepared are we to throw Constantine out and follow Jesus?

I once heard of a pastor who said this to his small church, "Our church will never be a big church. It will always be a small church. You know why? Because within 3 years I am going to train every one of you to become a church planter and then at the end of 3 years I am going to kick you out of this church to go and plant your own church somewhere else, and hopefully you will do the same with the church you plant. If I still see your face here in the 4th year, it means that I have failed. I have to give an account to God for everyone of you. Don't expect me to shepherd you for the next 25 years and marry you and bury you. If you don't want to be trained, I think you will be happier if you leave now."

If you think that is too radical then perhaps you are not ready to be part of the Kingdom. Jesus said He would rather we are hot or we are cold; not lukewarm, and He will spit out all those who are lukewarm (Rev.3:14-20).

Though I believe that "church planting" alone generally falls short of God's Kingdom mandate, yet to illustrate the point of multiplication I wish to share with you some of what is happening outside of "church as we know it". In India, a couple started a church in their house. They followed a simple strategy. They practiced personal discipleship. Every time it got up to about ten adults, they would split to become two house churches. Each house church formed will further spilt to become two house churches whenever they had about ten adults. Ten years have passed. There is no official count but it is estimated that in ten years more than 100,000 house churches have spawned from that one house church they started. Meanwhile the institutional church they were previously part of remains "church as we know it".

4. As a leader, how prepared are you to relinquish control and be a servant, and your church or group become a sailboat and be swept along by the wind of His Spirit?

The diagram on the next page illustrates two kinds of leadership. One is the kind we are all familiar with, practiced all over the world by politicians, governments, mafia, corporations, societies, and the institutional church. The other was practiced and modeled by Jesus. He said He came not to be served but to serve and to give His life for us. Then He actually did that. He was not interested in building a ministry. Paul followed Jesus. On average, he spent only 4 to 5 months in each place where he planted a church. Servant leaders empower and then disappear.

Jesus left behind no building, no organization, no institution, no staff, no money, no name, no corporate image and almost no disciples. At the end of His life, except for three Mary's and one John, all His disciples left Him. If we were standing there and watching the scene at Golgotha, would we think Jesus succeeded or He failed? Yet today we know that His Father looking down from heaven would have said, "Son, You totally succeeded!" By this we realize that God looks at success in a very different way from man.

Top-down leadership v. Servant leadership

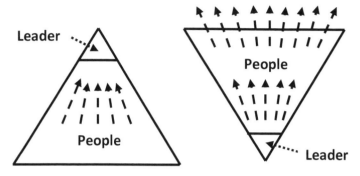

The people serve the leader and help the leader fulfill his calling.	The leader serves the people so that they go out and serve others and fulfill their calling.
Leader : "This is my calling. This is my vision. This is my dream. Help me succeed and you will be part of my success."	Leader : "What is your vision/dream/calling? How can I serve you and help you succeed? When you are successful, I have succeeded.
Result : Disempowerment and Redundancy	Result : Empowerment and Multiplication

"Jesus called them together and said, "You know that the rulers of the Gentiles lord it over them, and their high officials exercise authority over them. Not so with you. Instead, whoever wants to become great among you must be your servant, and whoever wants to be first must be your slave--just as the Son of Man did not come to be served, but to serve, and to give his life as a ransom for many." (Matt.20:25-28)"

* Believers, Seekers, the Indifferent, and the Antagonistic :

Jesus encountered all four in His time. When Jesus first started His ministry, He ministered to the crowds. Later it appears that He focused only on the believers and seekers. In fact He not only focused on them I believe *He filtered off all who were not true seekers and believers*. In John 6, after Jesus fed the 5000, He crossed over to the other side of the lake. The next day the crowds went to look for Him. When they found Him, He immediately told them, *"You are looking for Me because of the bread I gave you to eat."* That's what the Church is full off nowadays isn't it – people who just want God's blessings?

It is amazing what Jesus says next. He told them that they needed the Bread of Life and that He is the Bread of Life, and that unless they ate His flesh and drank His blood they would have no life in them. When they heard that, they could not accept it and all them, except the 12 apostles, left Him. Did Jesus not know that they had misunderstood Him – that they were taking Him literally about eating His flesh and drinking His blood? As they were all leaving, why didn't He stop them to explain to them what He really meant by that? Why did He let them all go away on a misunderstanding?

Then He turned to the 12 and asked them, *"Are you not leaving Me also?"*, almost inviting them to do so! Did Peter and the rest understand Jesus? I don't think they did either, but they were seekers and believers (except for Judas who was seeking something else). In their minds they were probably thinking to themselves, "Jesus, I have no idea either what You are talking about, but there's something about You, something that draws me to You and I am going to keep following You." Contrary to what many believe, God does not just want to populate heaven with "saved" people. He wants true disciples. Nothing less.

Appendix 1

Poverty Statistics

- 1.3 billion people live on less than one dollar a day
- 3 billion live on under two dollars a day
- 1.3 billion have no access to clean water
- 1.3 billion without adequate shelter
- 150 million with no shelter whatsoever
- 3 billion have no access to sanitation
- 2 billion have no access to electricity
- Approximately 790 million people in the developing world are still chronically undernourished, almost two-thirds of whom reside in Asia and the Pacific
- Every night more than 800 million go to bed hungry
- 500 million are on the verge of starvation
- There are 1.09 billion "absolute poor and destitute" defined as those whose existence is characterized by malnutrition, illiteracy and disease, and do not have access to basic health care, education and safe drinking water (230 million or 23% are Christians).
- UN research tells us : "Between 300 to 420 million people are trapped in chronic poverty. They experience deprivation over many years, often over their entire lives, and commonly pass poverty on to their children. Many chronically poor people die prematurely from health problems that are easily preventable. For them poverty is not simply about having a low income : it is about multidimensional deprivation – hunger, under-nutrition, dirty drinking water, illiteracy, having no access to health services, social isolation and exploitation. Such deprivation and suffering exists in a world that has the knowledge and resources to eradicate it."
- 1.4 million children die each year from lack of access to safe drinking water and adequate sanitation

- According to UNICEF, 30,000 children die each day due to poverty. And they "die quietly in some of the poorest villages on earth, far removed from the scrutiny and the conscience of the world. Being meek and weak in life makes these dying multitudes even more invisible in death." Every 5 seconds a child dies of hunger and related causes
- There are 246 million child laborers
- More than 1 million children join the sex trade each year.
- There are 120 million street children in megacities.
- There are 349 million homeless/family-less children.
- There are 670 million children who work to earn a living instead of being in school.
- 250,000 children will become permanently blinded this year for lack of a 10 cent vitamin A capsule or a daily handful of green vegetables.
- 17.4 per cent (37.4 million) of the Indonesian population live in extreme poverty. The Indonesian poverty line is the equivalent of US$12 per month which is far below the UN poverty line which is US$1 per day. If we take the UN poverty line, then 60 million are living in poverty. If we take the World Bank poverty line which is US$2 per day then 100 million or nearly half the population is living in poverty.
- We are on a downward spiral :
- In 1960, 20% of the world's people in the richest countries had 30 times the income of the poorest 20%. In 1997, it was 74 times.
- The income ratio between world's rich and poor countries 200 years ago was 1.5 : 1 In 1960 – 20 : 1, In 1980 – 46 : 1, In 1989 – 60 : 1
- The number of people living below the minimum poverty line (US$1/day) in Africa increased from 68 million in 1982 to 216 million in 1990

- There are currently one billion slum dwellers, but soaring urbanization will be behind the increase if it is not managed properly. The number of people living in slums will double to two billion by 2030 if urgent action is not taken. Worst hit is Sub-Saharan Africa where 72% of urban inhabitants live in slums rising to nearly 100% in some states.
- The richest 1% in the world owns 40% of the planet's wealth and the bottom half of the world's population owned barely 1% of global wealth.
- By 2015 Black Africa will have 332 million slum dwellers, a number that will continue to double every fifteen years.

What Churches Do With Their Money :

- 96% of all money given remains in the church
- 3% goes to work among the reached
- less than 1% goes to work among the unreached who are also the poorest people in the world

What Christians Do With Their Money :

- Out of the total annual income of Christians of $17.3 trillion :
- 99.9% of that is spent on ourselves
- 0.09% of that is spent on the evangelized non-Christian world
- 0.01% of that is spent on the unevangelized world

It costs less than US$70 billion a year (0.4% of the total annual income of Christians) to provide all people in developing and under developed countries with basic education, health care and clean water (which are the fundamentals for eradicating poverty) and yet poverty goes on unabated.

(Statistics were drawn from various sources including UN organizations, US Center for World Missions, Caleb Project, World Christian Trends, World Christian Encyclopedia, World Christian Database, Atlas of Global Christianity (Research Professors Dr David Barrett and Dr Todd Johnson)

Is it any wonder that many who profess to know Him will one day say to Him, "When did we see you hungry and thirsty and sick and naked ..?" If Jesus were to come again today, would you be found among the sheep or goats? When was the last time you helped a poor person or family?

Do these statistics not tell us how deceived and in bondage we are? Is that too radical a statement to make in the light of Jesus' command to love our neighbors as ourselves? And in the light of God's commands for the tithes to be used to feed the Levites, the fatherless, widows and aliens (refugees and IDPs)?

Someone said this : "It might well be that the greatest threat to human survival now confronting us is .. the loss of compassion. We are confronted daily with the pain of human tragedy ... to such an extent that we soon learn to turn off what we see. In order to cope with our feelings of helplessness, we teach ourselves how not to feel. The tragedy in this response which is probably more widespread than we dare to believe is that we also deaden our capacity for love. Almost everyone pities the poor, but only a few have compassion for them. Pity looks and feels but stops there. Compassion looks, feels and then does something. The difference between an ordinary Christian and a deeply committed one is that the ordinary Christian gets emotional while the deeply committed Christian gets involved."

Appendix 2

Chapter 1 from 'William Carey and The Regeneration of India' : by Ruth and Vishal Mangalwadi (reproduced with permission)

Imagine a quiz master at the finals of the All India Universities' competition. He asks the best-informed Indian students, **'Who was William Carey?'**

All hands go up simultaneously.

He decides to give everyone a chance to answer. The audience is asked to judge the correct answer.

'William Carey was the botanist,' answers a **Science student**, 'after whom *Careya herbacea* is named. It is one of the three varieties of Eucalyptus, found only in India.'

'Carey brought the English daisy to India and introduced the Linnaean system to gardening. He also published the first books on science and natural history in India such as *Flora Indica*, because he believed the biblical view, "All Thy Works praise Thee, O Lord." Carey believed that nature is declared "good" by its Creator; it is not *maya* (illusion), to be shunned, but a subject worthy of human study. He frequently lectured on science and tried to inject a basic scientific presupposition into the Indian mind that even lowly insects are not souls in bondage, but creatures worthy of our attention.'

'William Carey was the first Englishman to introduce the steam engine to India, and the first to make indigenous paper for the publishing industry,' pipes up the student of **Mechanical Engineering**. 'Carey encouraged Indian blacksmiths to make copies of his engine using local materials and skills.'

'William Carey was a missionary,' announces an **Economics major**, 'who introduced the idea of Savings Banks to India, to fight the all-pervasive social evil of usury. Carey believed that God, being righteous, hated usury, and thought that lending at the interest of 36-72% made investment, industry, commerce and the economic development of India impossible.'

'The moral dimensions of Carey's economic efforts,' the student continues, 'have assumed special importance in India, since the trustworthiness of the Savings Banks has become questionable, due to the greed and corruption of the bankers, and the nationalization of the banks, in the name of socialism. The all-pervasive culture of bribery has, in many cases, pushed the interest rates up to as much as 100 per cent, and made credit unavailable to honest entrepreneurs.'

'In order to attract European capital to India and to modernize Indian agriculture, economy, and industry, Carey also advocated the policy that Europeans should be allowed to own land and property in India. Initially the British Government was against such a policy because of its questionable results in the United States. But by the time of Carey's death, the same Government had acknowledged the far-reaching economic wisdom of his stand. Just as our Indian Government, after one-half century of destructive xenophobia, has again opened the doors for Western capital and industry.'

'William Carey was the first man,' asserts a **Medical student**, 'who led the campaign for a humane treatment for leprosy patients. Until his time they were sometimes buried or burned alive in India because of the belief that a violent end purified the body and ensured transmigration into a healthy new existence. Natural death by disease was believed to result in four successive births, and a fifth as a leper. Carey believed that Jesus' love touches leprosy patients so they should be cared for.'

The student of **Printing Technology** stands up next. 'Dr William Carey is the father of print technology in India. He brought to India the modern science of printing and publishing and then taught and developed it. He built what was then the largest press in India. Most printers had to buy their fonts from his Mission Press at Serampore.'

'William Carey,' responds a student of **Mass Communications**, 'was a Christian missionary who established the first newspaper ever printed in any oriental language because Carey believed that, "Above all forms of truth and faith, Christianity seeks free discussion". His English-language journal, *Friend of India*, was the force that gave birth to the Social Reform Movement in India in the first half of the nineteenth century.'

'William Carey was the founder of the Agri-Horticultural Society in the 1820s, thirty years before the Royal Agricultural Society was established in England,' says the post-graduate student of **Agriculture**. 'Carey did a systematic survey of agriculture in India, wrote for agriculture reform in the journal, *Asiatic Researches*, and exposed the evils of the indigo cultivation system two generations before it collapsed.'

'Carey did all this,' adds the agriculturist, 'not because he was hired to do it, but because he was horrified to see that three-fifths of one of the finest countries in the world, full of industrious inhabitants, had been allowed to become an uncultivated jungle abandoned to wild beasts and serpents.'

'Carey was the first man to translate and publish great Indian religious classics such as the *Ramayana*, and philosophical treaties such as *Samkhya* into English,' says the student of **Literature**. 'Carey transformed Bengali, which was previously considered "fit only for demons and women" into the foremost literacy language of India. He wrote Gospel ballads in Bengali to bring the Hindu love of musical recitations to the service of his Lord. He also wrote the first Sanskrit dictionary for scholars.'

'Carey was a British cobbler,' joins in the student of **Education**, 'who became a professor of Bengali, Sanskrit and Marathi at the Fort William College in Calcutta where civil servants were trained. Carey began dozens of schools for Indian children of all castes and launched the first college in Asia at Serampore, near Calcutta. He wanted to develop the Indian mind and liberate it from the darkness of superstition. For nearly three thousand years, India's religious culture had denied to most Indians free access to knowledge, and the Hindu, Mughal, and British rulers had gone along with this high caste strategy of keeping the masses in the bondage of ignorance. Carey displayed enormous spiritual strength in standing against the priests, who had a vested interest in depriving the masses of the freedom and power that comes from knowledge of truth.'

'William Carey introduced the study of Astronomy into the Subcontinent,' declares a student of **Mathematics**. 'He cared deeply about the destructive cultural ramifications of astrology; fatalism, superstitious fear and an inability to organize and manage time.'

'Carey wanted to introduce India to the scientific culture of astronomy. He did not believe that the heavenly bodies were "deities that governed our lives". He knew that human beings are created to govern nature, and that the sun, moon, and the planets are created to assist us in our task of governing. Carey thought that the heavenly bodies ought to be carefully studied since the Creator had made them to be signs or markers. They help divide the monotony of the universe of space into directions – East, West, North and South – and of time into days, years and seasons. They make it possible for us to devise calendars; to study geography and history; to plan our lives, our work and our societies. The culture of astronomy sets us free to be rulers, whereas the culture of astrology makes us subjects, our lives determined by our stars.'

A post-graduate student of **Library Science** stands up next. 'William Carey,' she reveals, 'pioneered the idea of lending libraries in the Subcontinent.' 'While the East India Company was importing ship-loads of ammunition and soldiers to subdue India, Carey asked his friends in the Baptist Missionary Society to load educational books and seeds into those same ships. He believed that would facilitate his task of regenerating Indian soil and empowering Indian people to embrace ideas that would generate freedom of mind. Carey's objective was to create indigenous literature in the vernacular. But until such indigenous literature was available, Indians needed to receive knowledge and wisdom from around the world to catch up quickly with other cultures. He wanted to make worldwide information available to Indians through lending libraries.'

'William Carey was an evangelist,' maintains the **student from the Indian Forest Institute**. 'He thought that "if the Gospel flourishes in India, the wilderness will, in every respect, become a fruitful field." He became the first man in India to write essays on forestry, almost fifty years before the Government made its very first attempt at forest conservation, in Malabar. Carey both practiced and vigorously advocated the cultivation of timber, giving practical advice on how to plant trees for environmental, agricultural and commercial purposes. His motivation came from his belief that God has made man responsible for the earth. It was in response to Carey's journal, *Friend of India*, that the Government first appointed Dr Brandis of Bonn to care for the forests of Burma and arranged for the supervision of the forests of South India by Dr Clegham.'

'William Carey,' argues a feminist **Social Science scholar**, 'was the first man to stand against both the ruthless murders and the widespread oppression of women, virtually synonymous with Hinduism in the eighteenth and nineteenth centuries. The male in India was crushing the female through polygamy, female infanticide, child marriage, widow-burning, euthanasia and forced female illiteracy, all sanctioned by religion. The British Government timidly accepted these social evils as being an irreversible and intrinsic part of India's religious mores. Carey began to conduct systematic sociological and scriptural research. He published his reports in order to raise public opinion and protest both in Bengal and in England. He influenced a whole generation of civil servants, his students at Fort William College, to resist these evils. Carey opened schools for girls. When widows converted to Christianity, he arranged marriages for them. It was Carey's persistent battle against *sati* for twenty-five years which finally led to Lord Bentinck's famous Edict in 1829, banning one of the most abominable of all religious practices in the world : widow-burning.'

'William Carey was an English missionary,' pronounces a student of **Public Administration**, 'who initially was not allowed to enter British India because the East India Company was against proselytizing of Hindus. Therefore, Carey worked in the Danish territory of Serampore. But because the Company could not find a suitable professor of Bengali for Fort William College, he was later invited to teach there. During his professorship, lasting thirty years, Carey transformed the ethos of the British administration from indifferent imperial exploitation to "civil" service.'

'William Carey,' reflects a student of **Indian Philosophy**, 'was a preacher who revived the ancient idea that ethics and morality were inseparable from religion. This had been an important assumption underlying the *Vedic* religion. But the *Upanishadic* teachers separated ethics from spirituality. They thought that the human self (*Atman*) was the divine

Self (*Brahma*). Therefore, our spirit cannot sin. Our *Atman* only gets deluded and begins to imagine itself as distinct from God. What we require is not deliverance from sin but enlightenment, i.e. a direct experience of our divinity. This denial of human sinfulness and emphasis on the mystical experience of our divinity made it possible for us in India to be intensely "religious", yet at the same time unabashedly immoral.'

Carey began to affirm that human beings were sinners and needed both forgiveness for sin and deliverance from its power over them. He taught that it was not ignorance but sin that had separated us from God; therefore, it was impossible to please God without holiness. According to him, true spirituality began only when we repented of our sin. This teaching revolutionized the nineteenth century religious scene in India. For example, after Raja Ram Mohun Roy, one of the greatest Hindu scholars of the nineteenth century, came in contact with Carey and the other missionaries at Serampore, he began to question seriously the spirituality then prevalent in India. He summed up his conclusions thus :

> "The consequence of my long and uninterrupted researches into religious truth has been that I have found the doctrine of Christ more conducive to moral principles, and better adapted for the use of rational beings, than any other which has come to my knowledge."

A student of **History** stands up last. 'Dr William Carey is the father of the Indian Renaissance of the nineteenth and twentieth centuries. Hindu India had reached its intellectual, artistic, architectural, and literary zenith by the eleventh century AD. After the Absolute Monism of Adi Shankaracharya began to sweep the Indian subcontinent in the twelfth century, the creative springs of humanity dried up, and India's great decline began. The material environment, human rationality, and all that enriches human culture became suspect. Asceticism, untouchability, mysticism, the occult, superstition, idolatry, witchcraft, and oppressive beliefs and practices became the hallmark of Indian culture. The invasion, exploitation, and the resulting political dominance of foreign rulers made matters worse.'

'Into this chaos Carey came and initiated the process of India's reform. He saw India not as a foreign country to be exploited, but as his heavenly Father's land to be loved and served, a society where truth, not ignorance, needed to rule. Carey's movement culminated in the birth of Indian nationalism and of India's subsequent independence. Carey believed that God's image was in man, not in idols; therefore, it was oppressed humanity that ought to be served. He believed in understanding and controlling nature instead of fearing, appeasing or worshipping it; in developing one's intellect instead of killing it, as mysticism taught. He emphasized enjoying literature and culture instead of shunning it as *maya*. His this-worldly spirituality, with as strong an emphasis on justice and love for one's fellows, as on love for God, marked the turning-point of Indian culture from a downward to an upward trend. The early Indian leaders of the Hindu Renaissance, such as Raja Ram Mohun Roy, Keshub Chandra Sen and others, drew their inspiration from William Carey and the missionaries associated with him.'

So, who was William Carey?

He was a pioneer of the modern missionary movement of the West, reaching out to all parts of the world; a pioneer of the Protestant Church in India; and the translator and/or publisher of the Bible in forty different Indian languages. Carey was an evangelist who used every available medium to illumine every dark facet of Indian life with the light of truth. He is the central character in the story of the modernization of India.

Appendix 3

What about the time when Jesus said, *"The poor you will always have with you and you can help them any time you want. But you will not always have me."* (Mk.14:7) ?

Did He mean that we are not to care about them and that we should care more for spiritual things? Surely not, because that would be inconsistent with His teaching on the parable of the sheep and goats and the parable of the Good Samaritan, and others like Lk.7:22 and Lk.14:13,21. See also Appendix 4 for Bible verses on God's heart for the poor.

Many people make the mistake of reading what Jesus said as a general principle, but He was actually addressing a specific situation. He was about to die and she was preparing for His burial, so they were not to make caring for the poor a distraction from what was immediately at hand. In fact, when Jesus said that, He was expecting the disciples to care for the poor and reminding them of their responsibility to do so later.

Appendix 4

God's Heart for the Poor

In the face of the overwhelming needs in the world and human suffering, what does the Bible have to say about the poor and needy? How does God feel about them? Here are some passages and references from the Bible :

- Matt.25 – the hungry, the thirsty, the naked, the homeless, the sick, the prisoner
- Deut. 15:4 – There should be no poor : God does not desire poverty
- Deut. 14:28-29, 26:12-14 – tithes for the Levites, fatherless, widows, aliens, sacred to the Lord
- Deut. 10:18-19 – God's love for the fatherless, widows and aliens
- Prov.19:17 – He who gives to the poor lends to the Lord
- Mark12:30 – love your neighbor as yourself : reflects the heart of God for the poor
- Lk. 16:19-25 – Rich man and Lazarus
- Lk. 10:25-37 – Parable of the Good Samaritan
- Lk. 14:13 – Banquet: Invite the poor, the crippled, the lame, the blind
- Lk.6:20 – Blessed are the poor, for theirs is the Kingdom of God
- Isa.61:1-4 – Anointing for the poor
- Isa.58:6-7 – The Lord's fast : to share your food with the hungry, to provide the poor wanderer with shelter, to clothe the naked
- Isa.1:17 – Encourage the oppressed, defend the cause of the fatherless, plead the case of the widow
- Jer.22:16 – Knowing God's heart reflected in defending the cause of the poor & needy

- Pr.31:8-9 – Speak up for those who cannot speak for themselves, for the rights of all who are destitute; defend the rights of the poor and needy
- Ps.82:4 – Rescue the weak and needy
- Ps.72:12-14 – God will deliver the weak, afflicted and needy. He will rescue them from oppression and violence, for precious is their blood in His sight.
- Duet. 15:7-11 – Don't be hard-hearted or tightfisted toward the poor and needy. Lend freely, give generously, be openhanded
- Gal.2:10 – to remember the poor
- James 1:27 – look after widows and orphans
- Acts 6:1-6 – aid to the poor, distribution of food
- Acts 11:29 – the Antioch Church responding to the famine in Judea
- Lev.25:35 – lend without interest, sell without profit
- Pr.3:28 – Do not say to your neighbor, "Come back later"
- Matt.5:42 – Give to the one who asks you, and do not turn away from the one who wants to borrow from you
- James 2:14 – Don't discriminate against the poor
- James 2:5-6 – God is for the poor
- James 5: 1-6 – Don't oppress the poor
- 1 Jn.3:17-18 – if anyone has material possessions and sees his brother in need but has no pity on him, how can the love of God be in him? Let us not love with words or in tongue but with actions and in truth
- The cry of the OT prophets against oppressing the poor, injustice against the weak and helpless, ignoring the plight of the poor and needy, etc.

Appendix 5

Saved But Not a Disciple?

Many Christians think that there are 3 categories of people : those who are saved and are disciples, those who are not saved, and those who are saved but not disciples. They are however mistaken. Neither Jesus in the Gospels nor anything in the epistles recognize or accept such a thing as being saved but not being a disciple of Jesus.

Jesus clearly equated salvation with entering into His Kingdom. See the passage on the rich young ruler : Matt.19:16-26 and others : Matt.7:21. Matt.8:11, etc. And He also talked about forsaking all and giving all to be part of His Kingdom : Matt.13:44-45. In other words, unless we forsake all and give all, we are not part of His Kingdom, and if we are not part of His Kingdom, we are not saved. So there is no such thing as being saved but not being a disciple of Jesus. You are either a disciple because you have forsaken all to follow Him (Lk.14:26-33) and have become a part of His Kingdom, or you are not part of His Kingdom and therefore not saved.

I heard Bob Weiner once put across this truth so powerfully. He asked all the women in the congregation, "Imagine you are about to get married next week and you are so excited about your wedding and this guy you are going to marry. Imagine if he comes to you and says to you, "Darling, I am so in love with you, and I can't wait to be married to you. I will love you 364 days a year; but just one day in a year, let me have a fling with my old girlfriend." Would you still marry him? Then he put the same scenario to the men and asked the men the same question. "Would you still marry her?" Then he asked all of us, "What makes us think that Jesus the Bridegroom will take us to be His bride and bring us into the marriage supper of the Lamb unless we are totally sold out to Him?"

Forsaking all is not about some kind of spiritual asceticism. It is about forsaking all other loves so as to be totally devoted to Jesus. It is also about denying ourselves to love others. Love always involves denying ourselves to put others first. When Jesus asked us to deny ourselves and take up our cross and follow Him, He was going to His death in His love for His Father and for others. *He was therefore calling us to deny and die to ourselves for others.* Denial of self has no meaning or virtue apart from love. What does it mean to be a disciple of Jesus? It means to follow Jesus. He gave up all to love people. So to follow Him is to do the same.

Unfortunately there are some who cannot accept this. They insist that once they believe and trust Jesus as their savior, they are saved and that's all there is to it. How they can ever explain away what Jesus said, *"Not everyone who says to Me "Lord, Lord" will enter the Kingdom of heaven, but only he who does the will of My father in heaven."* (Matt.7:21) is beyond me. In their mind, obedience, forsaking all, total commitment, love and good works is good but has nothing to do with salvation. Discipleship, according to them, is for those who want to commit their lives to Jesus, but it doesn't mean that if you are not totally committed to Jesus you are not saved. From their salvation by grace paradigm, what I am teaching is a false Gospel – a Gospel of Works.

I've heard those who hold this position tell me that the parable of the Good Samaritan and the parable of the sheep and goats in Matt.25 does not apply to Christians. They think that when Jesus was talking about the Good Samaritan, He was talking to the Jews. Not to us. Their reasoning is that at that time, it was still Old Testament time and Jesus was addressing the question of salvation from the Old Testament perspective of works. So that doesn't apply to us. And some think that Jesus was merely testing the expert in the law, to get him to see that he cannot fulfill the law so that he would depend on grace for salvation, not works.

As to the parable of the sheep and goats, they say Jesus referred to loving His brothers, not others. So it is about loving each other in the church. It is not about loving others outside of the church. Others think that the sheep and goats parable is applicable only to non believers, not to us. According to them, that is how Jesus will judge the non believers because Jesus talked about judging all nations gathered before Him. So the church will not be included in that judgment. They think there is a separate judgment for the church.

Allow me to clarify. Let me begin by asking, "If the parable of the Good Samaritan was only for the Jews for Old Testament time, what about John 3:16? What makes us think that that is for us, not just for the Jews? After all, in John 3:16 Jesus was talking to Nicodemus, a Jew. In fact in all of the Gospels He was talking to the Jews. If at that time it was still Old Testament time, then which part of the Gospels and which part of Jesus' teaching applies to us? And which part does not? And if the requirement to love our neighbors as ourselves is only for the Jews, why did Paul repeat it in Gal.5:14? And why did James repeat it in Jas.2:8?

Further, it is incorrect to think that salvation in the Old Testament was by works or by keeping the law. Paul took pains to expound clearly on that in Romans and Galatians and I shan't go into all of that here.

As to thinking that Jesus was merely testing the expert in the law, and that He wanted the man to fall back on God's grace, and not rely on works to save himself, why was there no statement or teaching from Jesus to the man to that effect? How would the expert in the law know anything about salvation by grace if Jesus did not tell him or clarify it to him? If that was what Jesus was implying, why then did Jesus tell the parable of the Good Samaritan? What was His point if not to clarify what love really means – not in terms of fulfilling certain criteria for salvation or doing good works to save ourselves but to be other-centered and see it from the point of view of people in need?

I'm sorry, but those who think that Jesus was only testing the expert in the law are not only unnecessarily reading more into the passage than its context allows, but they are missing the point. The irony is that those who do are in fact thinking of salvation from the works paradigm and interpreting everything from that paradigm. When you filter everything through that paradigm, even love will be regarded as works that someone needs to fulfill in order to be saved. Jesus was not telling him that in order to attain to eternal life he had to work for it. Instead Jesus was simply affirming that eternal life is synonymous with love. Eternal life is not about escaping hell. Eternal life is about not being separated from God but becoming one with Him, and if we are one with God we would love as He loves (see chap 3).

Love is not "works". But love is evidenced by action. If we really have love, that love will naturally result in action. When the Bible talks about loving others, it is not about loving others in order to save ourselves or secure our salvation. That is not true love. That is the requirement of some religions to gain merits for salvation. Love takes the focus off from ourselves and puts others as the center and sees things from the perspective of the other person. In fact to love our neighbors as ourselves is to first ask what it would be like if we were in the other person's shoes. Not law – as to what I must do to save myself, but love – as to putting the other person in priority to myself. Love in our hearts will cause us to emphatise with what the other person is going through. And if we truly love, obeying God comes naturally, and obedience will be evidence of that love. Jesus said :

^{JN 14:15} *"If you love me, you will obey what I command. ¹⁶ And I will ask the Father, and he will give you another Counselor to be with you forever-- ¹⁷ the Spirit of truth. The world cannot accept him, because it neither sees him nor knows him. But you know him, for he lives with you and will be in you.*

²¹ *Whoever has my commands and obeys them, he is the one who loves me. He who loves me will be loved by my Father, and I too will love him and show myself to him."*

^{JN 14:23} *"If anyone loves me, he will obey my teaching. My Father will love him, and we will come to him and make our home with him. ²⁴ He who does not love me will not obey my teaching."*

The obedience naturally comes out of God's love in your heart. You do not obey in order to prove your love. You obey because you love. It will in fact be a joy to obey.

Just as James says action is the evidence of faith, love is the evidence of a true relationship with God. It is not about fulfilling certain criteria in order to be saved. That would be operating under the law. Those who keep talking about salvation by grace through faith and insisting they are saved are missing the point. Not unlike how the Jews kept insisting they were children of Abraham notwithstanding Jesus telling them that their fruit showed otherwise and was conclusive evidence of their condition and who they really were. In other words, how we behave and live our lives is evidence of what is inside of us.

John the Baptist also said the same thing, *"Produce fruit in keeping with repentance … every tree that does not produce good fruit will be cut down and thrown into the fire."* (Matt.3:8-10)

John says those who do not love do not know God, no matter how much they claim to be saved and to belong to God. If a person is really and truly saved and has become a child of God, and God lives in him, then he would have the love of God in him and he would love people in need :

1JN 2:3 We know that we have come to know him if we obey his commands. 4 The man who says, "I know him," but does not do what he commands is a liar, and the truth is not in him. 5 But if anyone obeys his word, God's love is truly made complete in him. This is how we know we are in him: 6 Whoever claims to live in him must walk as Jesus did.

1JN 3:16 This is how we know what love is : Jesus Christ laid down his life for us. And we ought to lay down our lives for our brothers. 17 If anyone has material possessions and sees his brother in need but has no pity on him, how can the love of God be in him? 18 Dear children, let us not love with words or tongue but with actions and in truth. 19 This then is how we know that we belong to the truth, and how we set our hearts at rest in his presence 20 whenever our hearts condemn us. For God is greater than our hearts, and he knows everything.

1JN 4:7 Dear friends, let us love one another, for love comes from God. Everyone who loves has been born of God and knows God. 8 Whoever does not love does not know God, because God is love. 9 This is how God showed his love among us: He sent his one and only Son into the world that we might live through him. 10 This is love: not that we loved God, but that he loved us and sent his Son as an atoning sacrifice for our sins. 11 Dear friends, since God so loved us, we also ought to love one another. 12 No one has ever seen God; but if we love one another, God lives in us and his love is made complete in us.

God is love. Whoever lives in love lives in God, and God in him. 17 In this way, love is made complete among us so that we will have confidence on the day of judgment, because in

138

this world we are like him. ¹⁸ There is no fear in love. But perfect love drives out fear, because fear has to do with punishment. The one who fears is not made perfect in love.

1JN 4:19 *We love because he first loved us.*

So the question for each of us is, "What does our life show? Do we love our neighbors?" If not, we do not know God, and we are not saved. Because he who loves God will also love his neighbor. This is confirmed by the parable of the sheep and goats. When Jesus comes again, He will separate between those who were truly part of His Kingdom ("sheep" who loved) and those who weren't ("goats" who did not) : Matt.25:31-46. Our salvation is definitely linked to love of God and love of our neighbors, but not in terms of "love" as good works to earn our salvation. But if we are truly born again and have God's Spirit in us, then His love will be in us and it will be evidenced by good works. Jesus said that a tree is known by its fruit. If we are honest with ourselves and we know we do not love our neighbors as ourselves, meaning we do not have the love of God in us, meaning we do not really know God, and therefore we are not saved, then what should we do?

Those who are still stuck in the works paradigm will think that they need to quickly go out and love their neighbor in order to be saved. Or that I am telling them to do that. But that's really missing the point. The answer is not to go and prove your love, but to acknowledge that God's love is not in you. John says, *"love comes from God"* (1 Jn.4:7). Read that again! So the answer is to go to God and surrender yourself to Him and invite Him to come into your heart, and not to keep insisting that God is already in you (see Joe Ozawa's dream at the end of this book). If God is truly in your heart, you will have God's love and you will naturally love your neighbor as much as you love yourself.

But note this. Jesus said He and His Father will come and dwell in us if we obey, meaning the willingness and the decision to obey and the surrender has to come from us. God cannot do that for us. God will not force His way into our hearts. AW Tozer said that in everything between God and man there are two parts – God's part and man's part. Man cannot do God's part and God will not do man's part. We misunderstand grace if we do not see that grace calls for a response from man. Otherwise grace does not avail us.

James says, *"Draw near to God and He will draw near to you."* (Jas.4:8). God comes as close as He can without violating our will. Then He waits for us to respond. If we go to Him and acknowledge our sinful and bankrupt state, and ask Him into our hearts, He will. One of my favorite authors AW Tozer said that every man is as close to God and as full of the Holy Spirit as he wants to be. How close and how much depends not on God but on us. He longs to share His heart with us. But we must first decide to forsake all our idols and embrace Him fully. He cannot decide that for us. The problem of course is that people want to hang on to their idols. Jonah learnt that *"Those who cling to worthless idols forfeit the grace that could be theirs."* (Jon.2:8)

Next point, those who think the sheep and goats parable is to be confined only to the church, are implying that we don't need to love non believers as much. Does God love non believers less? Is it not Jesus who said,

"You have heard that it was said, `Love your neighbor and hate your enemy.' But I tell you : Love your enemies and pray for those who persecute you, that you may be children of your Father in heaven. He causes his sun to rise on the evil and the good, and sends rain on the righteous and the unrighteous. If you love those who love you, what reward will you get? Are not even the tax collectors doing that? And if you greet only your brothers, what are you doing more than others? Do not even pagans do that? Be perfect, therefore, as your heavenly Father is perfect." (Matt.5:43-48).

If God loved us and gave His Son for us while we were His enemies, that is the same love He wants us to have for our enemies. And if that is how we are to love even our enemies, then we should have the same love for everyone, believers and non believers.

As for the other view that the sheep and goats applies only to non believers, what does that mean? Are they saying that God requires more love out of non believers than He does out of His people? And are they saying that some non believers who love poor Christians will be accepted by Jesus as sheep without them accepting Jesus as their savior, and are they trying to say that one can somehow be saved by "good works"? You can see the fallacy of that kind of thinking I hope.

OK, back to the main point. Make no mistake that God wants all of our hearts. He has to be Lord of all. Any part of us that is not surrendered to God is a reserve unto ourselves that entrenches self there as lord and king in defiance of God. I once heard Jim Gilbert say that the simplest and most profound prayer that anyone can pray is to say to God, "You are God and I'm not." It is simply not enough to depend on God's grace for salvation but to retain control over our lives, or to have Jesus as our savior but not as our Lord.

I believe that the misunderstanding that most Christians have about salvation and discipleship stems actually from their lack of understanding of what the problem is, in the first place. When we do not understand the problem, we cannot understand the solution. That, I believe, is also why many Christians have misinterpreted and misunderstood Jn.3:16 (this was addressed in chapter 3). If we think the problem of man is just that he needs salvation because he has sinned, then Jn.3:16 and salvation is seen only as an escape from hell to go to heaven when we die. In order to understand the problem of man, we have to go back to the beginning to ask what really happened in the Garden of Eden.

The problem of man is not only that he disobeyed God but that he became his own god. Satan's half-truth "you will be like God" worked. Instead of listening to God, Adam made an independent decision to eat from that tree. When he received the knowledge of good and evil from that tree to discern for himself what was good or evil, and what was right or wrong, from that point onwards he no longer depended on God but relied on his own wisdom to decide things for himself. God was no longer his center. He became his own center. With the independent wisdom he now possessed and relied on, his independence was complete and he became his own god. That seed of independence, which is the essence of sin, has passed down to all of us.

For this reason Pr.3:5-6 says, *"Trust in the Lord with all your heart and lean not on your own understanding. In all your ways acknowledge Him and He will direct your paths."* To acknowledge Him is to say to Him, "You are God and I am not". That is what true repentance is. And we need to keep doing that in every situation we are in – to live a life of total dependence upon God. It is not enough that we just trust in Jesus as our saviour. The root of the problem, the sin nature in us, our lordship over our own lives, our self-centeredness, has to be dealt with. Jesus did not come just to save us from hell or just so that we will go to church every Sunday. There has to be a reversal or an undoing of what happened in the garden of Eden. For God's Kingdom to come, Man's kingdom must go. We cannot enter into God's Kingdom and continue being part of God's Kingdom without giving up our kingdom and dying to self. When we surrender ourselves to God we will become united with Him and His Spirit in us will empower and enable us to live the Christ-centered life. What is the Christ-centered life? If Christ is in us, then that love that compelled Him to lay down His life for us would also compel us to lay down our lives for others (1 Jn.3:16). That's why the test for whether we are truly in God's Kingdom, which is a Kingdom of love, is whether we are living for others and not living for ourselves. That's why John said that that is how we know if we have passed from death to life, and if we belong to the truth (1 Jn.3:14, 19)

I hope the point is now clear enough. It's not about we saving ourselves. Neither can we shirk or run away from surrendering all of ourselves to God. Instead, *salvation by grace includes God fulfilling His own law by living in us and through us – that is provided we allow Him, and continue to remain one with Him* (Rom.11:22). Read the uncompromising words of Jesus in John 15:1-13. Jesus made it abundantly clear that :

"I am the true vine, and my Father is the gardener. He cuts off every branch in me that bears no fruit …

I am the vine; you are the branches. If a man remains in me and I in him, he will bear much fruit; apart from me you can do nothing.

If anyone does not remain in me, he is like a branch that is thrown away and withers; such branches are picked up, thrown into the fire and burned …

This is to my Father's glory, that you bear much fruit, showing yourselves to be my disciples… If you obey my commands, you will remain in my love, just as I have obeyed my Father's commands and remain in his love… My command is this: Love each other as I have loved you. Greater love has no one than this, that he lay down his life for his friends."

Appendix 6

Ghana Story

In September 2007 after several months of drought, the rains arrived with force destroying homes and leaving crops underwater. According to the UN, 1.5 million African people were affected by flooding which hit a swathe of countries in West Africa. The Upper East Region of Ghana was one of the worst affected areas. As of September 21, 2007, official reports stated that over 90,000 people were displaced and nearly 20,000 homes were destroyed.

I was with Partners International. We had a partner ministry that has a church planting team in the north of Ghana. The communities in which they have been working were badly affected by the floods and thousands of people were out of food. They asked PI for help. Unfortunately, all PI could raise was $15,000. PI sent me there to give them a seminar on crisis response and help them determine what they could do with the $15,000.

When I got there, I told them that all we could raise was $15,000. I asked them what they would do with the money. Their first response was to buy food to distribute to the communities they were working in. I asked them how long that would last. They said about 2 to 3 weeks. At the very most, if they stretched it and everyone had only one meal a day, it could go up to 2 to 3 months. I asked, "So what would you do after that?" They said, "Well, we hope PI can raise more funds." I replied, "Sorry guys, I have been instructed that that's all we can raise. I'm sorry but please don't expect any more funds. If you give out bags of rice, the people will take the rice, thank you, and you won't see them again. Is there something you can do with the money instead to get the people together to work at something that can produce an income for them and some for you?

Each time they get together to work, they can cook and eat together and you will have continual access to build relationships with them … and that would be your church planting."

They were all pastors and church planters. They struggled to accept that getting involved in business was part of their church planting mandate. They said, "We are all Bible school graduates. We know nothing about business. And we were taught in Bible College to never get involved in business or money matters. We were told to engage strictly in church planting and nothing else besides that." I realized this was yet another group, typical of so many churches and mission groups that I had been encountering all over Asia where I have been giving training. They had a spiritual/secular dichotomy in their minds about ministry, or what Darrow Miller (Discipling Nations) calls "Evangelical Gnosticism". The problem as I see it, is the church has understood the Gospel only as the Gospel of salvation where the focus is heaven, and not the Gospel of the Kingdom that Jesus preached, where the focus is earth, where God desires for His Kingdom to reign and for abundant life and shalom to rule.

As with other places where I have been giving Community Development training, I asked them what they would do if a family in the village had a sick child that was dying, and the family was so poor they couldn't get the child to hospital. They responded that they would take the child to the hospital. I asked them, "Are you sure that is part of church planting?" They replied, "The Bible tells us to love people." I replied, "That's good, but why is the child sick in the first place? Why are all these kids falling sick in the villages?" They knew the answer. It was because of malnutrition and poor sanitation. I went on, "Why not do livelihood projects that will help the parents have income so they can feed their kids and have proper homes and sanitation and their kids would not fall sick in the first place? Is that not love? Why is "curing" love, but "prevention" not love? They replied, "We have never thought about that!"

While they were still thinking about it, I asked them if they ever visited people in prison. They said "Yes, we do." I asked them again, "Are you sure that is part of church planting?" They replied, "Jesus said when he was in prison "you visited me", so we should do that." I asked them, "Why are these people in prison in the first place, why do they get into gang fights and petty theft – is it not because the people are not gainfully employed? Would they get into crime if they were living purposeful lives? So how about helping people with livelihood and income so they would not get into prison in the first place? Is that not love? Why can you visit people in prison, but not help prevent crime? Why is curing more loving than preventing? They said, "This is a completely new way of thinking!"

After a lot more teaching on worldview and poverty and the Kingdom of God, they finally agreed that it was legitimate church planting activity to engage in business that would help resolve issues of poverty. Now the struggle was to know what to do. What could they do with $15,000 to really help the people? They had no idea. Again they said, "We know nothing about business." I said, "Well, I know nothing about your country and what you can do. But God knows what you can do with the $15,000. Let's pray and ask Him. In particular, let's pray that He gives us eyes to see and ears to hear. And we must decide on something by the end of this week when I leave." I had been teaching them that one of the things about poverty is that poverty blinds people from seeing what resources they already have from God. Instead, the people become dependent on outside resources and are always looking to the West for help.

The next morning I was in a vehicle with the leader. We were stuck in a traffic jam on the way to the seminar. In front of us was a truck loaded high with sacks of something. I felt a prompting from the Lord and I asked the leader, "What's in those sacks? He said, "shea nuts." I asked, "What are shea nuts? I've never heard of shea nuts. Are they for eating?" He said, "For making shea butter. That's the basic ingredient for making cosmetics." I was curious and asked further, "So the Japanese and Americans come here and buy the shea butter?" He replied, "Yes, Japanese, Koreans, Americans, Europeans .. they all come here." I asked, "So who owns the plantations that grow these shea nuts?" He replied, "No one. They are growing wild all over the northern part of Ghana." I was shocked. I exclaimed, "Hey this is the answer!" He replied, "What answer?"

I said, "Why not take the $15,000 and hire trucks and get the people from the communities to go and pick the shea nuts and buy a mill and grind them into shea butter and ..." He was excited. We got to the seminar place and he announced to all the participants that God had answered their prayer. After I left Ghana, they started doing just that. Many groups have been formed in different communities to produce shea butter. Later they even started a bakery among the women in a community, and I am told it is going well.

The point of the story is this. How could pastors and church planters divorce church planting and ministry from life itself? And how could they see love only in terms of helping when the problem had already arisen, not in terms of preventing it from arising? And how could they not see resources that God had already given them nor what to do with them? Was it not because they were focused only on the Gospel of salvation and they did not see their role as agents of God's Kingdom transformation in this world? And the church has nothing to do with the problems of this world?

Appendix 7

Why Paul's Theology Was So Salvation Focused

Often theologians who have been challenged to consider the ramifications of the Kingdom Gospel, have a question : Why was Paul so focused on his central theme of salvation by grace that it appears that he had little or almost no regard for a Kingdom Gospel or ministry? Could it be that the greatest apostle of all "missed" it, or that those of us who are now advocating for this paradigm shift are terribly mistaken? I have thought and prayed about that, and I could be wrong, but this is how I see it.

I believe Paul has been largely misunderstood by the evangelical world. This is how I believe we should read Paul : He was a Pharisee of Pharisees. He was zealous to the point of imprisoning believers and party to stoning Stephen to death. What would such a person do after he is knocked off his horse by Jesus and he discovers salvation by grace through faith, centered in the Person and work of Jesus Christ, and awakens to how terribly wrong he had been?

That question is like asking, "What would a drug addict who has been in and out of jail for petty theft and robbery do after he encounters Jesus, gets set free big time, and has a complete turnaround?" What would he become passionate about? Would he go and run a kindergarten or become passionate about translation of scriptures for unreached people groups or some other unrelated ministry? Surely he is going to storm right back into the world of drug dealing and drug addicts to try and free as many as he can from that kind of life!

It is so obvious from reading Acts and Paul's own epistles how nothing else was more passionate for him than wanting to see his new found discovery shared all over the place, especially for his own people. He said he could wish himself cut off for the sake of his brothers the Jews, if only they would have their eyes opened just like his eyes had been opened. I can imagine him so possessed with this one thing that he talks about almost nothing else except salvation in Jesus, to the point where the other apostles might have gotten a bit concerned about balance in Paul's ministry. It is no wonder we find this in Gal.2:10 : *"All they asked was that we should continue to remember the poor, the very thing I was eager to do."* Why else would they remind Paul about the poor?

The amazing thing is this. Paul knew Jesus had sent Peter to the Jews and him to the Gentiles (Acts 9:15, Acts 22:21, Gal.2:6-10), yet he couldn't quite get away from his focus (or might we say "obsession") on the Jews. Even after Jesus told him he was being sent far way to the Gentiles (Acts 22:21), (I can imagine why!), he was still constantly embroiled in heated arguments with the Jews right up to the end of his life (Acts 28:17-28). He himself told the Jews in Acts18:5-6 he was tired of them and that from then on he was going to the Gentiles instead. Yet a surprising thing happens later. Notice how in Acts 28:17 it was Paul himself who called the Jewish leaders together in Rome to meet with him and again he tried to convince them!

Doesn't this tell us why Paul's letters are full of the message of salvation and his ministry was so focused on that?

I am not saying Paul was not balanced, or that he missed it. Certainly not. It would be preposterous for anyone to even entertain such a thought. He was God's instrument for that time and God used him for the purpose of countering every other philosophy in the world at that time, and that would come after. And possibly no one else could expound on the centrality of Jesus in God's plan of salvation for all mankind like how Paul could. However, I believe it would be a mistake for us to take Paul's teachings and his ministry as the "be all and end all" of what the Gospel of the Kingdom is and its implications for ministry. That can only be Jesus.

We know that what Paul wrote in his epistles were responses to specific issues and not general treatises of his theology. Just like how we cannot read his epistles and come to the conclusion that Paul did not think spiritual gifts important because he addressed that subject only in Corinthians and nowhere else (and what a problem it created there!), so it would be better for us to stay away from spiritual gifts; it would be a mistake for us to jump to the conclusion that a seeming lack of an exposition by Paul on the subject of the Kingdom of God would mean he did not regard it as important. And in the same way we cannot try and figure out his whole theology on something and regard that as comprehensive, by extracting bits and pieces from his epistles, we must not read Paul and think that what he talked most about is all there is to the Gospel and ministry.

Although Paul taught on the Kingdom of God (Acts 19:8, Acts 28:23,31), there seems to be no record of exactly what he taught on that subject. It has been a mistake I believe to read his epistles as expounding on the whole of what the Kingdom of God means. As a matter of practice, Paul asserted that he was eager to care for the poor (Gal.2:10), and who among us would doubt he meant it? He also reminded the Ephesian elders in his last parting words, *"You yourselves know that these hands of mine have supplied my own needs and the needs of my companions. In everything I did, I showed you that by this kind of hard work we must help the weak, remembering the words the Lord Jesus himself said: `It is more blessed to give than to receive.' "* (Acts 20:34-35)

Ultimately, no matter how we look at Paul, I believe there is simply no substitute for going back to Jesus' teaching and ministry as the foundation, and looking at Paul as someone God has provided for us to understand more clearly some very important aspects of His plans and intentions for us.

Appendix 8

God's Love is Not Institutional – the Story of Danis

Danis is a Papuan from the Dani tribe. When the tsunami hit Aceh, he and a few Papuans felt the Lord calling them to go and help the people in Aceh. They arrived in Aceh in the first week after the tsunami. All around them they saw thousands and thousands of dead bodies, whole villages flattened or washed away and mountains of debris all over the place. It was like the end of the world had come. It was overwhelming to say the least. They wondered what they could do. They saw relief organizations with trucks of supplies with the logo of their organization on the sides of their trucks. These relief organizations had tents and houses and t-shirts and walkie-talkies. One relief organization even had helicopters.

Danis and his small team of 5 persons looked at themselves and said to each other, "God has given us hands and feet". So they went and helped to bury the dead. Danis himself buried about 200 dead bodies. He said in the first week it was smelly but it wasn't so bad. But it was terrible in the second week. By that time the corpses were rotting so badly that when he carried them, heads and arms and legs would fall off. He said that every day he had to throw away his clothes and he had to really scrub himself hard to get rid of the smell of rotting flesh. For food they got into line and queued up with the survivors. At night they slept in the tents along with the survivors.

After all the dead were buried, they wondered what they could do next. They looked at themselves and again they said, "God has given us hands and feet." So they helped to clean the place of all the debris. They cleaned out hospitals, public buildings, schools, the local mosque and people's homes. They worked day and night until they were totally exhausted each night when they went to bed. He told me, "As soon as we lay down we fell into a deep sleep within 2 seconds. Danis and his team became so well known for their outstanding work that the local government in Banda Aceh appointed Danis as the head of the cleaning up operations for the city. "It was just a title", he said, "there was no money to it". Nevertheless, they worked.

When all the debris had been cleaned out, they wondered what they could do next. Again they looked at themselves and again they said, "We still have hands and feet. Let's do what we can with what God has given us." So they started giving people massage and laying hands and praying for people. It was amazing what happened. People started getting healed! The news spread and many people came to get massaged and prayed for. Danis and his team were loved and received by the people, "despite the fact that we were black" said Danis.

One day Danis received news that his wife in Papua had passed away and he went back to Papua. For 8 months he was away in Papua. Then I heard that Danis wanted to return to Aceh but he could not afford an air ticket. I arranged for him to get an air ticket and I said to him, "Danis, can you bring me to meet all those families that you told me were "near to the Kingdom of God"?". He was very happy to do that. We got a van and he took me from house to house.

The first house we came to, he walked up to the front door and knocked. I stood behind him. When the door opened, an Acehnese woman stood there fully covered with the muslim customary jilbab. When she saw Danis, for a moment she was too shocked to say anything. Then she just burst into tears and embraced Danis repeatedly saying, "Danis, Danis, you have come back to us". I was totally amazed by what I saw. In all my 10 years in disaster relief, I have seen lots, and done all sorts of projects, but I have never seen anything like this. That I must say, was the most moving thing I have ever witnessed. Suddenly, the woman's husband came up from behind her. He too came up and embraced Danis with joy and with tears flowing down his cheeks.

We sat down to Acehnese coffee and some local cakes. I sat silently with tears streaming down my cheeks watching the love going on between them. I kept hearing the Lord saying, "This is my Kingdom."

The next house Danis brought me to, the same thing happened. And the next. And the next …

I went through a paradigm shift. I reflected on what I had been doing over the years and came to realize that all the people I had been helping had probably been seeing me as someone drawing a salary from a big organization or church and I was doing it as part of my job (although that was not the case). No doubt from how they were looking at me and what we were doing, they would think all the money for the project came from the "big" church or NGO that had sent me, not from me personally. How then could they feel my love? And how could they feel the love of an institution?

There was a big Christian NGO that was accused by the religious authorities of converting a young girl although it was not the staff of the NGO but their friends who befriended her. Despite having built thousands of houses for the survivors, no one stood up for them when the local authorities kicked them out of the area.

Some funds are needed no doubt, but I no longer think of raising big funds for disaster relief. Now I go around telling the story of Danis and telling people, "Big money causes big problems. No money, no problems. When they see the money, they don't see you anymore. And if they can't see you, how can they see God?" Neither has God called an institution to share His love. God has called us.

I now encourage people either as individuals or in twos or threes to personally go and partner with the poor. I don't have the last word on this, but this is how I currently look at it. There are 3 paradigms : the institutional church paradigm, the NGO paradigm, and the Kingdom paradigm. In the institutional church paradigm, the church says, "Give us your money and we will do the work". What work? The "spiritual" work. NGOs are saying the same thing, "Give us your money and we will do the work". What work? The work that the church is not doing – the social work. What I am saying is, "Why give your money to someone else to go and do what God has called you to do? Why don't you personally go and engage with the poor?" This is what I believe we need to return to – God's Kingdom paradigm – where love is personal, where you go and become friends with a poor family and see how you can help them do something that will generate income. Where they are lifted up to what they can become and not be perpetually dependent on aid.

There may be some of us who may be incapacitated in some way or for some reason are really not be able to go and get engaged personally with the poor and we therefore give to an NGO. That's great. Please do not misunderstand what I am saying. I am not in any way negating the wonderful work of NGOs who have been helping many poor communities in significant ways. I am merely questioning why you would push it off to others to do what God is calling you to do? Remember, the church is not the building, nor the denomination, nor the leaders, nor the committee. The church is you and your friends who love the Lord and want to share His love.

Jesus left His world to enter into our world and be with us. His name is Immanuel – God with us. In Jn.20:21, He said, *"As the Father has sent Me, I send you."* He sends us to do the same – to leave our world and enter into their world to be their friends and share our lives with them. If Jesus can come down all the way from heaven and lay down His life for us, is it too much for us to get across the city or even half way around the world to where the poor are and become their friends?

Appendix 9

Prayer and the Kingdom of God

There are several matters related to the Kingdom that I would like to address such as faith, and power and authority, and spiritual warfare, but to keep the message in this book concise I have omitted doing so. One thing however I must not leave out (though I left it out of the first edition of this book, and it has troubled me since), is about prayer. *"Your kingdom come, Your will be done, on earth as in heaven"* (Matt.6:10) does not only reveal God's desire for His Kingdom to reign on earth, but is also Jesus' instructions to us to pray for that to happen. The main message of this book has to do with our role in a far bigger scope of the Gospel than most believers realize. And love is central to the Gospel of the Kingdom. But we also need to pray – we need to agree with God for His will to be done on earth, or it will not happen.

Can God not act without us? John Wesley said that God will not do anything on earth except through prayer. He said that before God wishes to do anything He first finds someone to pray through for the thing to happen, for His will to be done, before He does it. Was John Wesley right? It has been said that prayer is one of those things which are mysteries which cannot be understood and it is best not to ask too many questions about it because there are probably no answers to it. "Just pray and hope for the best!" many say, "and maybe when we go to heaven we will find out the mysteries of prayer".

From the time I came to know the Lord at the age of 16, I was never satisfied with this kind of answer. Just as I needed an answer to why God put the tree of knowledge of good and evil in the Garden of Eden (See Appendix 10), I sought the Lord for an answer to why we need to pray. The two are of course related, and I believe what I said in Appendix 10 about that tree will also be in part an answer to why we need to pray – it has to do with the free will that God has given us, which I shall elaborate here. I don't claim to understand everything about prayer but I believe that if we only had a "maybe yes, maybe no" and "hope for the best" attitude towards prayer, then we are not going to be in a position to be channels for the Kingdom of God to advance. It is already well known and often said that the purpose of prayer is not to persuade a reluctant God to do something that might be against His will. And praying harder and adding fasting to it is not about trying to twist God's arm. It has also been said that prayer is not so much about trying to change anything, but that prayer changes us. I believe these convictions are true. However they do not really answer the question why we need to pray. They leave us still mystified about the purpose of prayer.

When we do not know the purpose of prayer, we will pray only in hope; not in faith. The Bible however does not teach us to pray in hope but to pray in faith. Neither can we pray in faith if we do not know the will of God for any situation. John said, *"This is the confidence we have in approaching God: that if we ask anything according to his will, he hears us. And if we know that he hears us--whatever we ask--we know that we have what we asked of him."* (1Jn.5:14). To "stay on the safe-side" some people always end their prayer with "Nevertheless not my will but Yours be done", or something to that effect. But that is not praying according to God's will. That reveals how unsure they are about what they are praying for. James tells us not to expect anything in response from God in that case (Jas.1:6-7) because that is not the kind of faith and confidence that John spoke of in 1 Jn.5:14. When Jesus prayed, *"Nevertheless not my will but Yours be done"*, He already knew what the will of God was in that situation (Matt.16:21). He was simply expressing His desire not to have to go through the cross and be separated from His Father if that was at all possible.

Moses' intercession with God in Exodus 17:9-11 is instructive of how prayer works. The Israelites were journeying towards the promised land. When they were in Rephidim, the Amalekites came and fought with them. While Joshua and his army fought with Amalek, Moses interceded with God on the top of a hill. When Moses held up his hand, Israel prevailed. But when Moses lowered his hand, Amalek prevailed. *God obviously desired Israel to prevail, but the fulfillment of God's came through Moses' intercession.* First, Moses raised his hands. Then God intervened from heaven. Then there was a tangible result on earth. What happened in the spiritual realm was governed by what took place first on earth. What if Moses had not held up his hands in intercession? No matter how much God willed for Israel to prevail, Israel would have been defeated. It is clear from this passage that it is not just God's will and action that's involved but also man's will and action. We cannot make God do what is contrary to His will, but it seems clear that we can hinder Him from doing what He desires to do.

I believe the key to understanding why we need to pray is found in Ps.115:16 : *"The highest heavens belong to the Lord but the earth He has given to man".* When God first created man, He intended for man to rule over all creation (Gen.1:26-27, Ps.8:4-6). God has given to man the responsibility to rule and to take charge of the earth. God is like a landlord who has leased the earth to us and given us the keys to its possession. Even though He continues to be the legal owner (Ps.24:1) yet like a landlord who respects his tenants right of possession, God will not come into our home unless we open the door to let Him enter. That is why Jesus said, *"Behold I stand at the door and knock .."* (Rev.3:20). We like to quote this verse to unbelievers but note that Jesus was speaking to the church when He said that, meaning that the church had kept Him out. As for each individual, though he may have accepted Jesus as his Savior, he may not have submitted to Him as Lord of his life. When Jesus comes into any part of our lives or any situation we invite Him to, He has to come in as Lord and King, not as servant to do our bidding.

Prayer therefore is opening the door and inviting Jesus to come into our hearts, into our world, and into our situation – into whatever situation we let Him and in submission to His will and purpose. Otherwise He remains outside. God gave man free will. Adam chose to be independent of God. Man continues to exclude God from his world. There are some things that even God cannot do or at any rate would not do. In His present creation and design, there is no such thing as a perfectly rounded square. To encroach on man's will would be to go against His very own design and negate the freedom of will He has given man. So God will not interfere with our lives, our affairs and our world and God will not intervene unless we want Him to. God waits until man desires His will and desires His intervention.

This is what I believe prayer is really about – a union between God and us which releases His will to be done on earth. This corresponds with the point that prayer changes us – it aligns us to God's will. Most people think that prayer is only about asking God to do something for us. The Bible does not restrict us in what we may pray for, but what I would like to draw our attention to – which involves another paradigm shift – is to see prayer not from our perspective, of what we want, but from God's perspective, of what He wants. This is about agreeing with God for His will to be done. In heaven there's only one will – all the angels and everyone in heaven and everything moves in accordance with God's will. On earth, there are billions of wills. In several places in Scripture we find God looking for people who would seek Him : Isa.59:15-16, Ezek.22:30, 2 Chron.16:9, Jn.4:23, Acts 13:22, 1 Cor.2:9-10. People are too busy minding their own affairs to care about what God wants. That is why Jesus taught us to pray, *"Your kingdom come, Your will be done, on earth as in heaven."* (Matt.6:10).

When Adam listened to Satan rather than to God, he surrendered his dominion to Satan and subjected himself to Satan's rule (Rom.6:16, Lk.4:6). But when man wills what God wills and submits himself back to God's rule, Satan cannot accuse God of trespassing upon his "turf" or territory or of infringing man's will. In this case man has opened a way for God to intervene (Isa.40:3-5). Prayer then, is not so much getting God to do what we want but asking God to do what He wants. When we choose God's will, we are exercising our free wills. It is God's will, but we choose it and therefore it is also our will. When there is such a union of our wills with God's will, God can freely carry out His will and it will not be an invasion of our wills and our lives. Instead when God carries out His will, He is doing what we really want.

In Matt.16:19 and Matt.18:18-19, Jesus said He has given to us the keys of the Kingdom of heaven. It has been pointed out by Bible scholars that the correct grammatical translation of the original Greek text of those two verses which are expressed in future-perfect passive participles, should actually read this way, "Whatever you bind on earth *shall have been bound* in heaven and whatever you loose on earth *shall have been loosed* in heaven." The binding, loosing and agreeing is effective only if they are executed or done on earth in accordance with that which has first taken place in heaven, after which there is a tangible result on earth. This corresponds to the intercession of Moses in Ex.17:9-11. God willed it from heaven first before Moses agreed with God in intercession for it to be done on earth.

This then is the prayer ministry of the church – to stand on earth for the will of man. When we pray, God does not just hear His church praying but man praying. This is the principle of intercession. God recognizes and accepts intercession because intercession is God's own divine way of effecting His mercy. Jesus' very coming to earth as a man and dying in our place was God's intercession for us to avert His judgment on us (Isa.53:12). Like Nehemiah we can identify with and stand in place of others and confess our sins as sinful men and plead God's mercy on us (Neh.1:4-11).

There are devotional prayers, and prayers of petition and all these have their place but they are no substitute for the kind of prayer that we, the church, have been charged with the responsibility and privilege of effecting. In Ezek.22:30, God said that because there was no intercessor He therefore poured out His wrath upon the land. If we only center our prayers on ourselves, on our personal problems, on little things that trouble and irritate us .. how can there be the way for the eternal purposes of God to get through? We cannot increase God's power but we can hinder it. We can restrict God by our apathy, our selfishness, our fear and caution, our smallness and our unbelief. The Israelites continually grieved God by their unbelief *and "limited the Holy One of Israel"* (Ps.78:41 NKJV). Jesus could not do many miracles in his hometown because of their unbelief (Matt.13:58).

Why does God wait for us? Why does God want us as His co-workers? I believe it is simply because He wants to restore us to what He created us for in the first place – to be in dominion (Gen.1:26). We could not do it by ourselves but Jesus' coming in the flesh as man and His death and atonement has made it possible (Rom.8:3-4, 1 Cor.15:45-57, Heb.2:14-15). When we align ourselves to God's will and by His strength we overcome in love and prayer, then we are restored to the position that God intended for us and one day we will rule with Him on this earth (Eph.2:6, Dan.7:27, Rev.5:10). Some would say that God wants us to already rule with Him now. This is where we need to get into the subject of authority and the "now but not yet" aspect of the Kingdom which is beyond the scope of this book.

How can we know the will of God for any situation? Many things are already clear in the Word of God – God is not willing that any should perish; Jesus came to destroy the works of the devil; Jesus came to give abundant life; Jesus came to set captives free, etc. He has revealed His nature and what He desires for us by His names – He is our provider, our healer, our deliverer, our guide, etc. God wants bring healing to the sick and blind and lame, to bring deliverance to the oppressed, to comfort those who mourn, to heal the brokenhearted, to give beauty for ashes, the oil of joy for mourning, the garment of praise for the spirit of heaviness. He sees the mess that the world is in. He sees all the injustices, the wickedness, the pain and suffering. He sees the millions and millions lost and heading for destruction. He sees the many things that keep people under bondage – animistic and occultic beliefs and other deceptive philosophies, and secular and humanistic structures and power struggles. He sees the pride and arrogance of man. God wants to bring His Kingdom down to earth. He desires for His truth and righteousness and love to reign on earth as in heaven – for His Kingdom to come into every situation. *God's will is just waiting to be released on earth and we have been given the keys of the Kingdom of heaven to unlock and release God's will to the earth.*

Apart from the general revealed will of God in scripture, it is when we draw close to God in prayer that we discover the specific will of God for any situation. Jesus said that His sheep hear His voice (Jn.10:27). How important then to approach God with open eyes to see and open ears to hear!

(Jn.5:19, Jn.20:21). Jesus said He would build His church upon the rock (foundation) of revelation that He gives to us (Matt.16:13-19).

Does it mean then that there is no point praying for anything unless we are sure it is within the will of God? I don't believe so. I believe that Mordecai's encouragement to Esther is the attitude we should adopt : *"Who knows but that you may have come to royal position for such a time as this?"* (Est.4:14). Who knows that what we are moved to pray in any situation might actually be the will of God that is just waiting to be released? It remains for us, like Esther who went into the king's presence, to get into God's presence and come into union with God for His will to be released on earth.

Will we always be able to discern God's voice? God's promise is that if we call to Him, He will show us great and mighty things which we know not (Jer.33:3). Perhaps the reason why we may still be unsure is because we do not seek enough or we do not press in enough until, like the woman with the issue of blood, we touch God and draw a response from Him (Mk.5:24-34). Imagine what this amazing woman had to fight and push through to get to touch Jesus. There was a physical barrier – Peter asked Jesus what He meant by *"Who touched Me?"* because the crowd was pressing in around Jesus and everyone was touching Him. Imagine her physical frame if she had been bleeding for 12 years and she had to push pass all the men (culturally only men would have crowded around Jesus) in order to touch Jesus. There was also the cultural barrier (women were not to touch men) that she had to push past. And there was also the religious barrier (she should not be even among the women : Lev.15:19-28) she had to overcome in her mind. No wonder it was only her touch that drew power from Jesus.

Jesus did not think we press in enough in prayer when He told the parable of the unjust judge and left us with the question, *"However, when the Son of Man comes, will he find faith on the earth?"* (Lk.18:8). How much do we want God's will to be done? That's the real issue at stake. Why is it often that we not only have to pray much but wait long before God's answers? I suspect that God often allows adversity and obstacles to try us so as to test us and bring out our heart's true desires. When despite all adversity and obstacles we still will God's will, that is when there's true union with Him. Indeed anyone who wills to will the will of God will discover that it involves not just his intellectual assent but also his entire person.

Apart from the clear teaching of scripture that unforgiveness blocks out answers to prayer, the other thing that might hinder answer to prayer is Daniel's account in Dan.10. He had been praying and fasting for three weeks before he got a breakthrough in prayer. An angel appeared to Daniel and explained to him that from the first day he had set his mind to seek the Lord, his prayer was heard and the angel had been sent in response but he had been held back by a principality called the prince of Persia; no doubt an evil personality. We are encouraged by James to pray through like Elijah, who was like nature to us, until we receive the answer to our prayer (Jas.5:16-18). Jesus exhorted us to be persistent in prayer like the friend who asked for bread at midnight and to keep on asking, seeking and knocking (Lk.11:5-13). See also Matt.15:21-28 on the persistence of faith of the Canaanite woman.

I am not trying to answer the question of why some prayers do not get answered. That is not my point or purpose. The main point I want to make is that we should not be deterred by unanswered prayers from persevering in prayer. Irrespective of whether God answers our prayer or otherwise, we are not to be discouraged. The writer of

Hebrews tells us to press on in faith despite the fact that we may not receive what is promised. He gives the example of many heroes of the faith who pressed on despite not having received the promise of God's promised Kingdom manifested on earth (Heb.11:13,39, Heb.12:1-3). Let's be encouraged by the Lord's own exhortation to us – men ought always to pray and not faint or lose heart (Lk.18:1). I believe that God's will and purposes are just waiting to be released through us. May we experience mighty breakthroughs in prayer. May His Kingdom come and His will be done on earth as in heaven. Come Lord Jesus!

(My understanding of God's part and man's part in prayer came through a very difficult and trying time sometime back. I was happy to discover later that it is similar to what Watchman Nee taught in his book – The Prayer Ministry of the Church)

Appendix 10

What About Suffering?
(And why did God put that tree there in the first place?)

From time to time when I teach on the Gospel of the Kingdom, listeners would ask, "What about suffering? If God loves us and wants His Kingdom on earth, why does He allow suffering? It doesn't make sense that God would send us to be agents of transformation so that things can be put right but at the same time He is letting things get out of hand. And why do bad things happen to even those who love and serve Him?

A complete answer to this question cannot be given in just a few pages as an appendix to this book. I may have to write another small book to answer this question. For now, I have to say this however. Please do not misunderstand what this book is about. If you have read up to this point in the book, I trust you would have come to understand that this book is not just about some kind of utopia on earth. I am not saying that God wants us all to have a nice and comfortable world to live in that is free of all suffering. That is absolutely not my point. My purpose rather is to challenge us into a paradigm shift from a self-centered personal-salvation heaven-focused Christianity to a God-centered neighbor-loving (especially the poor) Kingdom of God on earth focused Christianity.

So why then did I talk about being agents of change or transformation? The objective is not about changing this world to make it a better world or about the absence or eradication of suffering in this world. Please note that I am not advocating transformation without the Kingdom or the King. We are called to be salt and light to reflect the glory of our Father, and influence others with God's Kingdom culture and values so that His Kingdom – His love, truth and righteousness will reign everywhere. Yes being salt and light will mean transformation, but it is not a vision for transformation that should motivate us. Instead it is love for God and love for our neighbor.

Why did God put the tree of knowledge of good and evil in the Garden of Eden in the first place? Didn't He know that Adam and Eve will fall for Satan's temptation, and didn't He know the terrible consequences of sin and suffering that will result? Of course He did! And there is no doubt He purposely allowed and indeed planned for that to happen. Contrary to what most Christians believe, the Bible is clear that the fall of man into sin and Jesus' coming to earth as savior was not an afterthought rescue plan but was pre-planned and ordained by God from the very beginning. God Himself subjected the whole of creation to frustration in hope that the creation itself will be liberated from its bondage to decay and brought into the glorious freedom of the children of God (Rom.8:20-21).

It is through pain and agony, and through trials and suffering that God will purify and refine for Himself those who will look like Him, walk like Him, think like Him, feel like Him and even smell like Him (Rom.8:17-21, 28-30). That is what God is after. A more adequate explanation will have to wait until I come out with a book on it, but for now I will just say this : One of the best things that God can do for us is to allow suffering into our lives. This may appear to contradict what I said earlier in this book, but I assure you it does not.

Until the fullness of God's Kingdom comes, I believe that in the face and in the midst of all the sin, wickedness, sicknesses, poverty, accidents, disasters, etc. and with all our limitations, our present life on earth is both a test as well as an opportunity to learn His love. God created us in

His image to become like Him. But the full potential of becoming like Him cannot happen unless we are given the power of choice. Love is not something that can be programmed in us. Love is not love unless it comes out of a heart that is free to choose. So God gave us choice. But choice means little until it is tested. That is why God put that tree there. Adam and Eve and all of us would have to be tested. One day the perfect will come. Meanwhile the world would be put to the test – what would each of us choose?

It is while we live in the imperfect, and while our knowledge and understanding is partial (1 Cor.13:9,12), that we are tested and we can also learn to love. It is when we choose to reach out in love despite being wronged, or despite being falsely accused, or misunderstood, or despised, or when we are in want or suffering lack ourselves, that we unite with God's desire for us and by His Spirit we are changed to become more like Him. The angels and the whole of creation are waiting to see who in the end will be revealed as the children of God (Rom.8:18-21).

God's end goal for us is not happiness but that we become transformed to become like His Son, to become like Him, which is why He created us in the first place (Gen.1:26, Rom.8:28-30). To mould and shape us to become even more like Him, there is nothing better that God can do than take us through suffering to break us, and to whittle away and burn up the self in us (Jn.15:2, 2 Cor.12:7-10, Heb.12:1-12). But it is God's sovereign right to accomplish His purposes through suffering (Rom.8:16-39), and it is for us to reach out in love to those who are suffering.

How can we love despite being wronged, or despite being falsely accused, or misunderstood, or despised, or when we are in want or suffering lack ourselves? How can we, like Jesus, lay down our lives for others? (1 Jn.3:16). And how can we do that if we ourselves are carrying hurts and need to know God's love and healing for ourselves in the first place? I would like to share with you an account of a dream that Joe Ozawa (whom I regard as my mentor) had many years ago. He tells it in his own words in his coloring book for kids "The Hippopotamus Postman" :

"One day while asleep, I had an unusual dream. Maybe it was a vision? I found myself suddenly before God in heaven. How did I know it was God? I couldn't see His face, but it was like looking straight at the sun. So very bright. Only, it wasn't a burning feeling. Only a sense of great love and a power I didn't understand.

I fell to my knees and began to apologize for myself. In fact, I didn't quite know what to apologize for, but I figured that if this really was God, it would be a really smart thing to begin our conversation with my apologies.

"Oh God, I'm sorry that I have not prayed enough," I said weakly.

"Well, that's very important, but that's not the most important thing," He said in return in a very deep, rich voice.

"Then, well....yes, I'm so sorry that I eat too much. You know I can't help myself sometimes. I know I should be fasting more, but I can't seem to do it," I apologized.

"Well, that's very important, but that's not the most important thing," He said.

I began apologizing for everything I could think of. What else could I have done wrong? Maybe I didn't give enough money to the poor? Maybe I didn't have enough faith? Then a thought came to me.

"Oh God, I know now. I haven't been very nice to my wife. I know I should love her better. That must be it!"

"Oh, that's very, very important, but that's not the most important thing," He said once again.

"Oh God, oh God, what do you want from me anyway?" I asked, whining like a little spoiled child. He was really frustrating me! I just couldn't figure Him out. What did He want from me anyway?

"When you appear before me the final time, I will only have one question to ask you......" (Now to this day, I still don't know exactly what "the final time" means).

"When you appear before me the final time, I will only have one question to ask of you......

DID YOU LEARN TO RECEIVE MY LOVE?

Then He said, "Now, go tell this to the world!"

With that, He waved His big, big hand and sent me flying through the air..... (like an astronaut flying through outer space) and I landed back on my bed with a thud! I turned to my wife. "Honey, guess what happened? I just went to heaven," I said loudly. "Tell me tomorrow morning," she replied, rolling over and going back to sleep.

Please write this down, and remember that phrase, "Did you learn to receive My love?" for I'm convinced that one day, you too will be asked that question about God's great love for you."

Bibliography

Books that have especially impacted me :

1. Wolfgang Simson, *Houses that Change the World,* OM Publishing, 2001.

2. Wolfgang Simson, *Starfish Manifesto,* https://whileweslept.wordpress.com/2009/10/27/starf ish-manifesto/

3. Darrow L. Miller, *Discipling Nations : The Power of Truth to Transform Cultures.* YWAM Publishing, 1998

4. Scott D. Allen and Darrow L. Miller, *The Forest in the Seed : A Biblical Perspective on Resources and Development.* Disciple Nations Alliance, 2006

5. Darrow L. Miller, *Life Work : A Biblical Theology for What You Do Everyday,* YWAM Publishing, 2009

6. Bryant L. Myers, *Walking With the Poor : Principles and Practices of Transformational Development,* Orbis Books, 1999

7. Bert M. Farias, *Soulish Leadership : Whose Kingdom Are You Building?,* Treasure House, Destiny Image Publishers, Inc., 1998

8. John White, *The Cost of Commitment*, InterVarsity Press, 1976

9. A W Tozer, *The Pursuit of God,* Christian Publications, 1957

10. AW Tozer, The Knowledge of the Holy, New York : Harper & Row, 1961

11. AW Tozer, *That Incredible Christian,* OM Publishing, Bromley, Kent, 1989

12. George Verwer, *Hunger for Reality,* STL Books, 1979

13. Watchman Nee, *The Normal Christian Life,* Gospel Literature Service, 1957

14. Watchman Nee, *The Release of the Spirit,* Christian Fellowship Publishers Inc, 2000

15. Watchman Nee, *The Spiritual Man*, Christian Fellowship Publishers

16. Scott Peck, *The Road Less Traveled,* TOUCHSTONE, Simon & Schuster, 1978

17. E M Bounds, *Power Through Prayer,* Moody Press, 1989

18. Gene Edwards, *A Tale of Three Kings,* Tyndale, 1980

19. Rick Joyner, *The Final Quest,* Morningstar Publications, 1997

20. Rick Joyner, *The Call,* Morningstar Publications, 1999

21. Editors Ralph Winter & Steven Hawthorne, *Perspectives on the World Christian Movement, A Reader,* William Carey Library, 1999

22. Juan Carlos Ortiz, *Disciple,* Charisma House, 1975

23. Ruth and Vishal Mangalwadi, *William Carey and the Regeneration of India,* Good Books (Mussoorie), 1997

24. Ravi Zacharias, *Deliver Us From Evil,* W Publishing Group, 1997

25. Joe Ozawa, *The Hippopotamus Postman,* Alby Commercial Enterprises, 1998

The "heavier" books for a wholistic theology of the Kingdom :

1. Editors Vinay Samuel & Chris Sugden, *Mission as Transformation : A Theology of the Whole Gospel*, Regnum Books Int. 1999

2. David Bosch, *Transforming Mission : Paradigm Shifts in Theology of Mission,* Orbis Books, 1991

3. Christopher J.H. Wright, *The Mission of God : Unlocking the Bible's Grand Narrative,* Inter Varsity Press, 2006

4. Christopher J.H. Wright, *The Mission of God's People : A Biblical Theology of the Church's Mission,* Zondervan, 2010

Made in the USA
Charleston, SC
22 October 2015